MICROSOFT® EXCEL® *for* ACCOUNTING PRINCIPLES

MICROSOFT® EXCEL® *for* ACCOUNTING PRINCIPLES

KATHERINE T. SMITH
Business Consultant

L. MURPHY SMITH
Texas A&M University

LAWRENCE C. SMITH, JR.
Louisiana Tech University

PRENTICE HALL
Upper Saddle River, NJ 07458

Acquisitions editor: Diane deCastro
Executive editor: Annie Todd
Editor-in-chief: P.J. Boardman
Editorial assistant: Fran Toepfer
Production manager: Richard Bretan
Manufacturer: Victor Graphics

Microsoft and Windows are registered trademarks of the Microsoft Corporation
in the U.S.A. and other countries. This book is not sponsored or endorsed by or
affiliated with the Microsoft Corporation.

Smith, Katherine, T.
     Excel for accounting principles / Katherine T. Smith, L. Murphy
  Smith, Lawrence C. Smith, Jr.
        p.   cm.
     Includes index.
     ISBN 0-13-013567-4
     1. Microsoft Excel for Windows. 2. Accounting--Data processing.
  3. Electronic spreadsheets I. Smith, L. Murphy.   II. Smith
  Lawrence C.   III. Title.
HF5548.4.M523S653 1999
657'.0285'5369--cd21   99-17434
                                                             CIP

Printed in the United States of America

10   9   8   7   6   5   4   3   2   1

Prentice-Hall International (UK) Limited, *London*
Prentice-Hall of Australia Pty. Limited, *Sydney*
Prentice-Hall Canada Inc., *Toronto*
Prentice-Hall Hispanoamericana, S.A., *Mexico*
Prentice-Hall of India Private Limited, *New Delhi*
Prentice-Hall of Japan, Inc., *Tokyo*
Prentice-Hall (Singapore) Pte Ltd
Editora Prentice-Hall do Brasil, Ltda., *Rio de Janeiro*

TABLE OF CONTENTS

DEDICATION

To the students who use this book. We hope each of you will enjoy the true success which is measured by moral character and personal integrity. "A good name is more desirable than great riches; to be esteemed is better than silver or gold" (Proverbs 22:1).

To our children: Hannah, Jacob, and Tracy. "Children are a gift from God; they are His reward" (Psalm 127:3).

To our parents: Genita and Hubert Taken, and Doris and Junior Smith.

KTS & LMS

To Doris Elaine Barfoot Smith, my beautiful wife. "A worthy wife is her husband's joy and crown" (Proverbs 12:4).

To the memory of D. Gray Miley, the consummate professor.

LCS

ACKNOWLEDGEMENTS

The authors are grateful for the contributions to this project made by Paul Ashcroft, Tracy D'Alessandro, Diane DeCastro, Marilyn Fuller, Sharon Hurley Johns, Rick Myers, Judy Moore, and Dave Woytek. Additionally, the authors appreciate the support and encouragement they have received, over the years, from Russell Briner, Dot Davis, Dena Johnson, Danny & Susan Ivancevich, David Kerr, Paul Kochanowski, Stan Kratchman, Jeff Miller, Steve McDuffie, Uday Murthy, James H. Packer III, Grover Porter, Steve Salter, Jim Sena, Phil Siegel, Bob Strawser, Carol Sullivan, and Jim Thompson.

STUDENT DISK

The student disk included with this book includes a number of helpful example files. These include the following:

Gledger	Includes general ledger accounts which are linked to the trial balance and income statement.
Incstmt	Basic income statement.
Piechart	Basic pie graph.
Graph	Four graph types.
Bep	Cost-volume-profit analysis (break-even point) with graph.
Ratio	Financial ratios.
Demsup	Economic demand and supply analysis.
Profit	Microeconomic analysis of profit-maximizing equilibrium.
Macro	Example of a macro used to sort a range of data.

For updates, example files, and other helpful information, check the Web site (http://www.IOL19.com/murphy/excel/).

Microsoft Excel
for Accounting Principles

INTRODUCTION

The purpose of this book is to introduce accounting students to the fundamental tools and techniques available in Microsoft Excel™ spreadsheet software. Applications are presented that pertain to specific accounting principles topics. Assignments may be selected from those contained within the book or from others provided by the instructor.

The book provides detailed instructions for using Microsoft Excel 97. These instructions are sufficient for most other versions of Excel, as well. The student disk accompanying this book includes a number of example files. Additionally, solutions to odd-numbered exercises 1 through 45 are provided in this book (but not on disk). Thus, if the instructor assigns these exercises, the student will know exactly how the completed assignment should appear.

WEBSITE

For updates, example files, suggested assignment schedules, and other helpful information, check the Web site (http://www.IOL19.com/murphy/excel/).

Computer Basics 1

This chapter briefly describes components of the personal computer, operating systems software, Windows, and starting your spreadsheet program.

COMPONENTS OF THE COMPUTER

As shown in Exhibit 1.1, the basic personal computer system consists of a monitor, keyboard, and a central processing unit (CPU). The CPU consists of three components: main memory, arithmetic logic unit, and supervisory control. Main memory includes random access memory (RAM) and read-only memory (ROM). The RAM of a typical personal computer may be as little as 640 kilobytes (K) or as much as 128 megabytes (MB). The box or chassis containing the CPU also contains other devices such as the graphics card which connects to the monitor, a parallel port which connects to a printer, a serial port which connects to a mouse, a modem which connects to the phone line, a hard disk drive which provides secondary storage (typically ranging from one to four gigabytes), a floppy disk drive, and a CD-ROM drive.

Floppy disk drives include the 3 1/2 inch, 1.44 MB (high density); 3 1/2 inch, 720 K (double density); 5 1/4 inch, 1.2 MB (high density); and 5 1/4 inch, 360 K (double density). The 3 1/2 inch high density drive is the most common.

The keyboard on your computer is made up of three basic sections: the function keys, the numeric key pad, and the alphanumeric keys. The alphanumeric keys, the main part of the keyboard, include letters, numbers, and a variety of symbols. The function keys, labeled F1 through F12, have different uses depending on the software currently in use.

The numeric pad is located on the right side of your keyboard. A significant key on the numeric pad is the NUM LOCK key, which is a toggle key that enables the user to switch between the number keys and the cursor control keys located on the numeric pad.

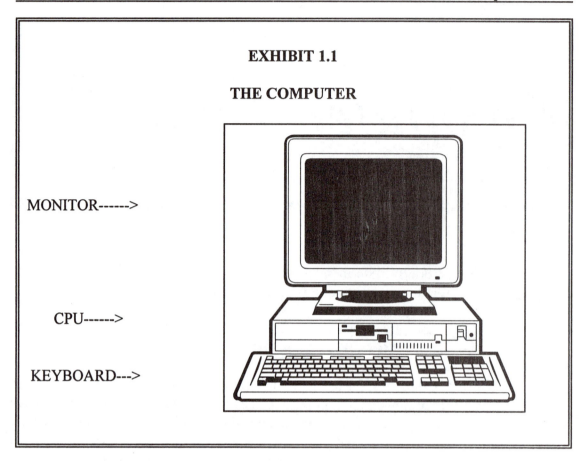

EXHIBIT 1.1

THE COMPUTER

MONITOR------>

CPU------>

KEYBOARD--->

OPERATING SYSTEMS SOFTWARE

An operating system runs your computer and manages your computer's activities. The operating system of the personal computer functions much like the operating systems on the mainframe or minicomputer. For the IBM-compatible system, there are three operating systems available. Currently, the most popular is Microsoft's Windows 98. The second most widely used is Microsoft's Disk Operating System (MS/DOS). Another is a joint venture system offered by IBM and Microsoft, called OS/2. The Apple Macintosh has an operating system called System 7.

For any system, software shells can be imposed over the operating system. The shells are called when the system is initialized, making the operating system transparent to the user. It appears to the user of such a system that the shell is the operating system interface. They become the presentation system for operation of the PC. One such shell that operates on the PC-compatible system is Windows 3.1. In 1995, Windows 3.1 was replaced by Windows 95, a true operating system. In 1998, Microsoft released Windows 98.

Windows is a set of software programs that provides a graphical user interface similar to that of the MAC. When running Windows, the computer user interacts with the computer visually and by use of a mouse rather than typing commands. Two kinds of programs can be run under Windows -- the standard DOS applications and Windows-specific applications which are designed to take advantage of Windows' special capabilities.

WINDOWS OPERATING SYSTEM

The most prominent feature of Windows is the use of icons (little pictures) to represent programs or groups of programs. After Windows is loaded (running), you run programs such as Excel by moving the pointer to the icon and double-clicking the left mouse button. A program icon represents a "shortcut" in Windows 98 and 95, and a "program item" in their predecessor Windows 3.1.

WINDOWS 98

Microsoft periodically upgrades its Windows program. The current release is Windows 98. The Windows 95 operating system provided many user-friendly enhancements to its predecessor, Windows 3.1. Windows 98, like Windows 95, uses "folders" and "shortcuts." A folder may contain several shortcuts (which access specific programs such as Excel or Lotus 1-2-3). Each folder has a menu bar which allows creation of shortcuts or folders within that folder (select "File"-"New").

As programs are run, an icon appears on the bottom menu bar of the display screen. This provides immediate access for switching between programs that are being used simultaneously. Also on the bottom menu bar is the "Start" menu icon. By clicking on "Start," you are given various options such as Run, Find, Settings, Programs, etc.

Additional information for Windows may be obtained from the "Help" function. Simply click on the menu-bar choice "Help" to initiate this process.

WINDOWS 3.1

Program Manager is the chief Windows 3.1 program. In Windows 3.1, all program groups are contained within Program Manager. By double-clicking on program group icons, you are provided access to the individual programs (i.e., program items) in that group. Program Manager has a menu bar with several choices: File, Options, Window, and Help. For example, by clicking on "File," the screen will display a submenu containing several choices such as New, Open, Delete, Run, and Exit Windows. By clicking on "New," you can add new program groups or program items. "Run" can be used to run any DOS or Windows-based program. Typical program groups include the following: Main, Start-Up, Accessories, Applications, Games, etc.

Within the "Main" program group is a very useful program named "File Manager." The actual program is "Winfile.exe" but it is typically labeled "File Manager" when the program item is set up. The File Manager program allows you to view directories by clicking on "file folder" icons. It also may be used for many useful tasks such as opening files, moving files, deleting files, etc. To accomplish these tasks, you must first click on "File" which is the first item on the File Manager menu bar located at the top of the screen.

STARTING YOUR EXCEL SPREADSHEET PROGRAM

Excel by Microsoft Corporation is the most widely used spreadsheet software. In order to start Excel, follow these steps:

1. In Windows 98, use your mouse to click on the "Start" button on the bottom left side of your computer screen. The button should expand into a box with several options for selection.

2. From the Start menu, select the Programs options, which will open another box with options. If Microsoft Excel is listed separately, double-click the Excel option to open (run) the program. If there is not a separate listing for Microsoft Excel, then scroll to the Microsoft Office option and select Microsoft Excel.

OR

*   If an Excel icon is shown on screen, simply double-click on that icon.

SPREADSHEET ORGANIZATION

Once the spreadsheet software is loaded (as explained in Chapter 1), a screen or one similar to it appears as shown in Exhibit 2.1. The spreadsheet you see is called a worksheet in Excel. Each Excel file, called a workbook, can hold several worksheets. The worksheet display includes rows, columns, a control panel, mode indicator, and cell pointer.

ROWS AND COLUMNS

On the worksheet, there are letters across the top and numbers along the left side. Each letter refers to a column and each number refers to a row. The intersection of a column and a row is referred to as the cell location. Cell A1 is highlighted in Exhibit 2.1. Cells are where data, either text or mathematical expressions, are entered.

CELL POINTER

The cell pointer is like a cursor; the highlighted cell indicates your current location on the worksheet.

MENU BAR

In Microsoft Excel, almost every command that you perform can be "launched" from the Menu Bar. The Menu Bar is located at the top of the worksheet. As you can see from Exhibit 2.1, the Menu Bar is made up of several different "menus" such as File, Edit, and Help. The array of menus will vary depending on your version of Excel. You can access each menu by simply clicking on it with your mouse or by pressing the ALT key and the

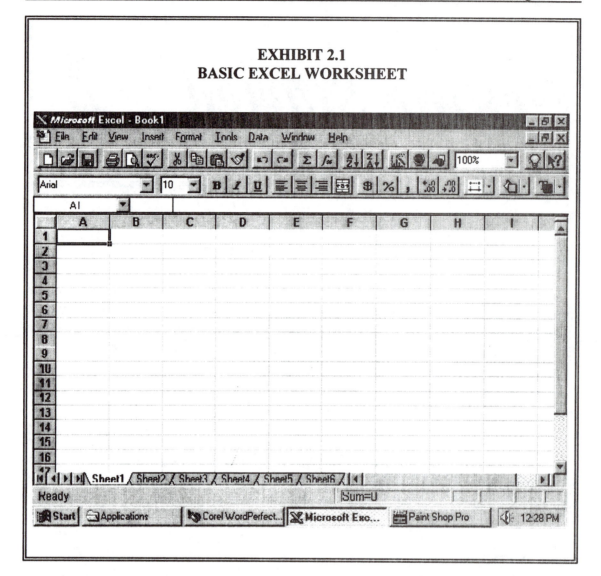

EXHIBIT 2.1
BASIC EXCEL WORKSHEET

underlined letter in that menu simultaneously. For example, to access the File menu, you can either click on File in the menu bar or press the ALT key and the F key simultaneously. When you access each menu, a number of options will appear from which to choose. Each menu has different options and as you begin to choose within a menu, the menu bar may change to show you commands that specifically relate to that option.

TOOLBAR

As shown in Exhibit 2.1, the icons or buttons underneath the Menu Bar at the top of the worksheet make up your toolbar. In the newer versions of Excel, there are two rows of buttons in the toolbar. If you hold the pointer on a button for a second, it will state what its function is. By simply clicking on the button, the function will be performed. For example, to print an Excel worksheet, you would click on the print button (the icon of a printer). The functions of each button will be explained in more detail in Chapter 4.

AN EXAMPLE

To begin your familiarization with Excel worksheets, we will work through an example worksheet using just the essential commands. The commands in creating a worksheet file include: saving files, printing files, closing files, and retrieving files. Step-by-step instructions to accomplish these commands will be provided. Throughout this book, you will typically have the option of perfoming a task using either the menu bar or the toolbar buttons; instructions for both are usually provided.

You will now create a worksheet using the data below. Assume that you work in the accounting department at a local grocery store. Your boss has requested a breakdown of sales by department, comparing the last two years.

	A	B	C	D	E
1			ABC Store	Sales	
2					
3			12/31/01	12/31/02	
4	Produce				
5	Bakery				
6	Dairy				
7	Deli				
8	Meat				
9					

To start, click on cell C1 with your mouse and type in "ABC Store." When finished typing, press Enter or click on another cell; the typed data will automatically be inserted into the worksheet. Now click on cell D1, type in "Sales," and press Enter. Another way to move among the cells is to use the arrow keys. Proceed to type in the remaining data from the example given. Note that column B is left empty to give extra spacing for the purpose of improving the appearance of the worksheet.

SAVING

When you have entered all the information, save your worksheet using the following commands:

1.   Choose the File menu and select the Save-As option.
2.   The Save-As menu box will appear and the name "Book1" will be highlighted in the file name box. Delete that name and enter a new filename, such as "Example." If you are using Windows 95 or 98, you may choose up to 255 characters or spaces for the file name. If you are using an earlier version, you must limit the file name to eight characters; spaces are not allowed. Eight-character file names are recommended.
3.   In the "save in" box (located in top left of Save-As menu box), click on the down arrow to select the directory in which you want to save the file, such as A-drive (your floppy disk) or C-drive.
4.   Click on the OK or Save button.

Now that you have named your worksheet, you can save it with a simple:

*   Click on the "Save" button in the toolbar (icon of a floppy disk):

PRINTING

Print your worksheet using the following commands:

*   Click on the "Print" button on the toolbar (icon of a printer):

OR

1.   Choose the File menu and select the Print option.
2.   Make sure all options are set up correctly (i.e., set to the right printer and the correct number of copies selected).
3.   Click on the OK button.

To view your worksheet before printing, use the following commands:

*   Click on the "Print Preview" button in the toolbar (the icon of a sheet of paper with a magnifying glass over it).

OR

1.   Choose the File menu and select the Print Preview option.
2.   If the worksheet looks exactly like you want, then click the Print button.
3.   To cancel the print command, click on the Close button.

CLOSING FILES

When you are finished with your work, you need to close your file. After saving your worksheet, close the Excel file as follows:

* Click on the "X" button in the upper righthand corner of the menu bar on your worksheet.

OR

1.   Choose the File menu and select the Close option. (As a safeguard, the program will ask if you want to save the changes you made.)

RETRIEVING FILES

To retrieve a worksheet and bring it up on the screen, use the following commands:

* Click on the "Open" button in the toolbar (icon of an open folder):

Type the file name into the upper file name box, or simply double-click on the file name as shown in the listing and this will automatically enter it into the upper box.

OR

1.   Choose the File menu and select the Open option.
2.   Type the file name into the upper file name box, or simply double-click on the file name as shown in the listing and this will automatically enter it into the upper box.
3.   Click on the OK or Open button.

EXITING

After you have saved and closed your file, you can exit the Excel program as follows:

*   Click on the "X" button in the upper righthand corner of the screen (this appears above the "X" button used for closing the worksheet).

                            OR

1.   Choose the File menu and select the Exit option.

Editing   *3*

While working on a spreadsheet file, you may want to edit a particular cell or even the entire worksheet. Several commands are discussed in this chapter that will enable you to alter the appearance of an individual cell or the entire worksheet. Exhibit 3.1 displays the sales worksheet originally introduced in Chapter 2, but with values added for each year. Enter the values into your worksheet. Note that Excel automatically right-justifies a number after it is entered into a cell. (If you have already closed the file, retrieve it by clicking on the toolbar button with the picture of an open file. As discussed in Chapter 2, type your file name into the upper file name box, or simply double-click on the file name as shown in the listing and this will automatically enter it into the upper box.)

EDITING A CELL

If you discover a mistake after you have already entered data into a cell, the function key **F2** will put you back into the edit mode. F2 enables you to edit data within a cell. Click the cell pointer on the cell you wish to edit, press F2, and the cell's contents will be displayed in the control panel just above your worksheet. You can move within the control panel by using the arrow keys and change the contents of the cell by using the Delete, Backspace, and other keys. After editing, press Enter, and the revised contents will appear in the worksheet. If you want to erase the **entire** contents of a cell, you can do so without using F2 by simply clicking on the cell and then pressing the Delete or Backspace key.

MOVING CELL CONTENTS

To move the contents of a cell, first click on the cell you wish to move. Position your pointer on the bottom right corner of the cell until the pointer turns into a white arrow. Hold down the left mouse button and drag the pointer to the new cell. Release the mouse button, and the contents will appear in the new cell.

EXHIBIT 3.1

SALES BY DEPARTMENT WORKSHEET

	A	B	C	D	E	F
1			ABC Store	Sales		
2						
3			12/31/01	12/31/02		
4	Produce		100	150		
5	Bakery		300	450		
6	Dairy		250	375		
7	Deli		125	200		
8	Meat		125	175		
9						
10						

EDITING A WORKSHEET

INSERTING ROWS AND COLUMNS

Referring to Exhibit 3.1, suppose you want to insert a row between the dates on row 3 and the Produce sales figures on row 4. The row can be inserted as follows:

1. Position your cell pointer accordingly. Rows are added **above** the cell pointer, so click on any cell in row 4.
2. Select the Insert menu. (In older versions of Excel, you will have to first choose the Edit menu and then select the Insert option.)
3. Choose Row to insert. Click on the OK button if necessary.

As shown in Exhibit 3.2, row 4 is now blank and the sales figures begin on row 5.

Suppose you want to insert a column between the dates (columns C and D) in order to show the change in sales from one year to the next. Columns are added to the **left** of the pointer, so to add the column in our example, click on any cell in column D. Select the Insert menu and choose Column. Column D is now blank while the latest sales figures have been moved to column E. Type the heading "Change" into cell D3. Exhibit 3.2 shows the new column formation. The change in sales was entered manually in this example; Chapter 5 explains how to install formulas so that the Excel worksheet will automatically perform computations such as this.

EXHIBIT 3.2

SALES BY DEPARTMENT WORKSHEET #2

	A	B	C	D	E	F
1			ABC Store	Sales		
2						
3			12/31/01	Change	12/31/02	
4						
5	Produce		100	50	150	
6	Bakery		300	150	450	
7	Dairy		250	125	375	
8	Deli		125	75	200	
9	Meat		125	50	175	
10						

CUT AND PASTE

This command enables you to move the contents of one cell or cells to another cell or cells within the worksheet. Anything already in the receiving cell will be deleted, so make sure that the new location does not contain any valuable information you want to keep. Using the worksheet shown in Exhibit 3.2, suppose you want Bakery to be listed last. To move Bakery from cell A6 to A10, follow these steps:

* If you have an Excel version with Cut and Paste icons: click on the cell which contains the data you want to move, in this case, cell A6 containing "Bakery." Then click on the Cut button (scissors): ✂

    The data has been "cut" out of your worksheet and saved in a temporary file called the clipboard. The data will remain in that temporary clipboard file until you replace it with new data. A rotating line will encircle the data until you paste it into a cell.

Next, click on the cell in which you want the data pasted (A10 for our example). Then, click on the Clipboard (paste) button: (Some programs use an icon of a paste bottle.)

OR

1. Click on the cell you want moved. Then choose the Edit menu and select the Cut option.
2. Now click on the cell in which you want the data placed. Choose the Edit menu and select the Paste option.

Instead of moving the Bakery sales amounts one cell at a time, you can cut out cells C6, D6, and E6 all at one time. Hold down the left button on your mouse as you move the pointer over cells C6 through E6. The cells have now been highlighted. Click on the Cut button. Next, highlight cells in which you want the data placed (C10, D10, and E10.) Click on the Clipboard button. The Bakery sales amounts have been moved. Any number of rows or columns can be cut and pasted at one time. Note: row 6 can be deleted since it is now blank (instructions are below). When you delete row 6, Excel will automatically renumber the rows. Exhibit 3.3 displays the worksheet with these changes.

DELETING ROWS AND COLUMNS

To delete rows and columns, use the following commands.

1. Excel will delete the column or row in which the cell pointer is currently located, so click on the column or row you want deleted.
2. Choose the Edit menu and select the Delete option.
3. Choose to delete the Entire row or the Entire column. (Click on the OK button if needed.)

COPY AND PASTE

Instead of cutting out and removing the contents of a cell, this command allows you to copy the contents of a cell and duplicate it into another cell. The original cell remains the same. Using your worksheet, suppose you want the name of the store displayed in cell A3 as well as in cell C1. Execute the following steps.

EXHIBIT 3.3

SALES BY DEPARTMENT WORKSHEET #3

	A	B	C	D	E	F
1			ABC Store	Sales		
2						
3			12/31/01	Change	12/31/02	
4						
5	Produce		100	50	150	
6	Dairy		250	125	375	
7	Deli		125	75	200	
8	Meat		125	50	175	
9	Bakery		300	150	450	
10						

---

*   Click on the cell which contains the data you want to duplicate; in this case it is cell C1 containing "ABC Store." Then click on the Copy button (icon of two sheets of paper).

Next, click on the cell in which you want the data pasted (A3 for our example). Click on the Clipboard button.

You can paste the data in as many locations as you like without repeating the copy step. A rotating line will encircle the data until you perform a different function.

If your Excel version does not have the copy icon, first click on the cell you want copied, then choose the Edit menu and select the Copy option. Now click on the cell in which you want the data placed. Choose the Edit menu and select the Paste option. Exhibit 3.4 displays the worksheet with the copy and paste change along with changes from the following paragraphs.

The newer versions of Excel provide a shortcut method of copying a cell into an adjoining cell (this works only for adjoining cells). Simply click on the cell you wish to copy. Position the pointer in the bottom right corner until the pointer turns into a black "+." Hold down the left mouse button and drag the pointer to an adjoining cell or cells. Release the mouse button and the data will be copied.

SELECTING CELLS

Multiple cells can be cut, copied, and pasted by selecting or highlighting a range of cells instead of a single cell. You have already had some practice in this when you moved the Produce data. To select a range of cells, hold down the left button on your mouse as you move the pointer over the desired cells. The cells will be highlighted or darkened. Then proceed with the usual commands of the function you desire. Cells can be unselected by clicking on an area that is not highlighted.

CENTERING

Data within a single cell can be centered by clicking on the cell and then clicking on the toolbar button which displays centered lines. Suppose you want to center the entire heading on the worksheet -- ABC Store Sales. Delete the cells in which they are currently located. (Do this by clicking on the cell and pressing Delete.) Retype the entire heading into cell A1. It will expand beyond the border. We want the heading to be centered between columns A and E, so select (highlight) row 1 from A to E. Then click on the toolbar button with the boxed in "a" (merge and center button). The heading should now be centered as shown in Exhibit 3.4.

CHANGING COLUMN WIDTH

When the spreadsheet program is first loaded, the column width will be eight characters. Columns can be made wider or smaller depending on your needs. Suppose you want to tally the total sales for each year. You want to put the heading "Total Sales Per Year" in column A. This heading is obviously longer than eight characters, so widen column A by using the following commands:

* Column widths can be changed by using the mouse. Position the cursor at the top of the screen on the mid-point between the column headings (between A and B in this case). The cursor should change into a "+." Click-and-drag using the left mouse key; hold it while "dragging" the column to a greater width.

OR

1. Click on any cell in Column A.
2. Choose the Format menu and select the Column option.
3. Select the Width option and a box will appear to allow you to change

the column width. Enter the width you want the column to be in terms of the largest number of characters you'll be placing into a cell in that column.

4. Click on the OK button.

If your cell data exceeds the cell width, the data will simply overflow into the next cell **if** the next cell is empty. However, if the next cell is not empty, the overflow data will be truncated at the cell border.   Exhibit 3.4 displays the worksheet with an elongated column A. Save this worksheet, it will be used in Chapter 4.

EXHIBIT 3.4

SALES BY DEPARTMENT WORKSHEET #4

	A	B	C	D	E	F
1			ABC Store Sales			
2						
3	ABC Store		12/31/01	Change	12/31/02	
4						
5	Produce		100	50	150	
6	Dairy		250	125	375	
7	Deli		125	75	200	
8	Meat		125	50	175	
9	Bakery		300	150	450	
10	Total Sales Per Year					

Excel Commands 4

This chapter presents basic information concerning toolbar buttons, the keyboard and mouse, and function keys of Excel. Shortcuts are explained using these devices.

TOOLBAR BUTTONS

You have become familiar with some of the buttons on the toolbar by working through the examples in Chapters 2 and 3. As you have discovered, they are simple and efficient. Using our example "Sales by Department" worksheet from Chapter 3, practice using the following toolbar buttons.

AUTOMATIC SUMS

The newer Excel versions have a toolbar button with the Greek sigma sign (Σ). This button is called "autosum" and will automatically sum numbers within cells you select. Now let's total the departmental sales. If you recall, to select a range of cells, hold down the left mouse button while dragging the pointer over the desired cells. For example, click on cell C5 and drag the pointer down to cell C9. The cells in this range will darken. Click on the autosum button. The total will automatically be inserted into the next cell. Repeat this for the other columns.

To place an underscore in a cell; first, click on the cell to be underscored, then click on the underscore button (U). Do this for cells C9, D9, and E9. Exhibit 4.1 displays the totals along with changes from the following paragraphs.

CURRENCY STYLE

To further dress up our worksheet example, let's add dollar signs. The toolbar button with the icon of a dollar sign is called "currency style" and will automatically add a dollar sign, decimal, and cents places to any cell you select. Since our example contains a whole column of figures, remember to select the range of cells instead of clicking on them one by one. After you have selected the cells, click on the dollar sign button. For future use, Chapter 5 will explain how to achieve other variations in currency formats. Your worksheet should now look like Exhibit 4.1.

SORTING WORDS AND NUMBERS

Using our example worksheet, suppose we want the departments in alphabetical order. On the current version of Excel, there is a button displaying the letters A and Z along with an arrow. It is called "sort ascending" and will automatically alphabetize a list going from A to Z. In our example, we want to sort the departments along with their corresponding sales amounts, so you must select all the appropriate cells. To achieve this, click on A5 and hold the left mouse button down while you drag the pointer across to E9. Once the cells are selected, click on the sort ascending button. Your worksheet should now look like the one shown in Exhibit 4.1. Note: you will have to move the underscores.

The sort ascending button can also be used on a list of numbers, reordering them from smallest to largest. However, if there are words included in the cells you've selected, Excel will give the words priority over the numbers and alphabetize the words only.

EXHIBIT 4.1
SALES BY DEPARTMENT WORKSHEET

	A	B	C	D	E	F
1			ABC Store Sales			
2						
3	ABC Store		12/31/01	Change	12/31/02	
4						
5	Bakery		$ 300.00	$ 150.00	$ 450.00	
6	Dairy		$ 250.00	$ 125.00	$ 375.00	
7	Deli		$ 125.00	$ 75.00	$ 200.00	
8	Meat		$ 125.00	$ 50.00	$ 175.00	
9	Produce		$ 100.00	$ 50.00	$ 150.00	
10	Total Sales Per Year		$ 900.00	$ 450.00	$ 1350.00	
11						

Exhibit 4.2 describes other commonly used toolbar buttons in Excel.

EXHIBIT 4.2
MICROSOFT EXCEL TOOLBAR BUTTONS

Button	Name	Action
	Help	Click once for help on your current activity. Click twice to bring up the Help menu.
	Open	Brings up an existing Excel file.
	Save	Saves a file. It is wise to save your work often in case of a computer malfunction.
	Print	Brings up the print menu. Then simply press the Enter key to print your worksheet.
	Cut	This removes (cuts out) selected data from a worksheet and saves it on the Clipboard. From there, you can place or "paste" it anywhere on your worksheet.
	Copy	This makes a copy of selected data and saves it on the Clipboard so it may be pasted elsewhere.
	Paste	Takes data from the Clipboard and pastes or places it in the selected cell on a worksheet.
	Undo	Cancels or undoes the last action you did.
	Repeat	Repeats your last action.
	AutoSum	Adds the numbers from a selected range.
	Function Wizard	Leads you through the process of entering a function in your current cell.
	Chart Wizard	Leads you through the process of creating an Excel chart.

There is also a "sort descending" toolbar button with the picture of a Z on top of an A. Obviously, it sorts words from Z to A. It can also be used to sort a list of numbers from largest to smallest.

KEYBOARD

Various keys on the keyboard enable you to navigate around a worksheet file. Common functions are listed below, along with instructions for accomplishing them.

CANCEL AN ACTION

Pressing the Ctrl and Scroll Lock keys cancels any action, i.e., printing, sorting, etc.

ESCAPE

Pressing Esc will back you out of the current menu selection; thus, you escape from the process.

PAGE UP/PAGE DOWN

Pressing the Page Up key or the Page Down key allows you to move up or down one page in the same column.

FUNCTION KEYS

There are function keys at the top of the keyboard which are labeled F1 through F12. Some of the keys have no purpose. Below are some useful function keys.

KEY	COMMAND	FUNCTION
F2	Edit	Edits cell contents
F5	Go to	Moves the pointer to a specified file, worksheet, or cell. This is helpful when working with a large file or worksheet.
F7	Spelling	Runs SpellCheck on the open worksheet file.

Formatting, Formulas, and Functions 5

The following example will be used throughout this chapter to illustrate formatting and functions. Create a new worksheet by clicking on the worksheet icon (top left of screen display). If you need to first remove your worksheet from the previous chapter, click on the "X" in the upper right corner of the worksheet. Assume that you are asked to prepare a worksheet to calculate loan payments based on the information below. Type the following information onto your worksheet.

	A	B	C	D	E	F
1	Rate		0.10	0.05	0.05	0.06
2	Years		10	20	15	8
3	Principal		100000	30000	80000	20000
4	Annual Payment					

You will note that "Annual Payment" extended into column B on your worksheet. This was feasible since column B was empty. However, the better approach is to widen column A in order to accomodate all data. You will recall from Chapter 3 that the easy way to widen column A is to position the pointer on the mid-point between the A and B column headings at the top of the screen. The pointer should change into a "+." While holding down the left mouse button, drag the column to the desired width. Later in this chapter, we will calculate the annual payment using an Excel function.

FORMATTING

NUMERIC FORMATTING

The general steps on formatting numeric data will be explained along with specific steps for the example. You can format an entire worksheet or just a group of cells within the worksheet. Exhibit 5.1 shows the options available for numeric formatting.

EXHIBIT 5.1
EXAMPLES OF AVAILABLE NUMERIC FORMATS

Format Type	Display
Number	123 1,234 1,234.56 -1,234.56 or (1,234.56) With the number format, you can choose commas, decimals, and negative numbers.
Date	May 31, 1999 5-31-99 31-May-99 May-99 There is also an option to have the time displayed with the date.
Percentage	5% or 5.00% You can determine how many decimal places to use.
Currency	$123 $1,234 $1,234.56 $(1,234.56) You can choose whether the negative amounts appear in black or red. You can also choose other types of currency.

The general steps for numeric formatting are given below, followed by specific instructions regarding the example worksheet. First, select the cells that need formatting. (Remember, in order to select and highlight cells, hold down the left mouse button as you move the pointer over the cells you want selected.)

* With the current version of Excel, click on the icons displaying a dollar sign, comma, or percentage symbol, depending on which is required. (More explanation is given below.)

OR

1. Choose the Format menu and select the Cells or Number option.
2. In the Category box, choose either Currency, Percentage, or Number. (Note: You also choose the number of decimal places desired.)

Using the example data, format the cells containing the rates by first selecting cells C1 through F1. If you have the current version of Excel, simply click on the icon which displays the percentage symbol. The numbers will be converted to percentages without decimal places. For older versions of Excel, choose the Format menu and select the Cells or Number option. In the Category box, choose Percentage. Select the format with zero decimal places. After you click on OK, the percentage signs will be inserted in the selected cells.

To format the cells containing the principal, you must first widen columns C, D, E, and F in order accommodate more than eight characters. Look at Exhibit 5.2 to get an idea of how large the columns need to be. Next, select cells C3 through F3. If you have the current version of Excel, simply click on the dollar sign and comma icons to format the cells. For older Excel versions, choose the Format menu and select the Cells option. In the Category box, choose Currency. Select the format with dollar signs, commas, and two decimal places. In some Excel versions, dollar signs and commas are automatically inserted; you select the number of decimal places desired.

The years in this example are simple enough; they do not need formatting. However, if you had many large numbers, the cells could be formatted to automatically insert the commas and/or decimal places.

Your worksheet should now appear as follows:

	A	B	C	D	E	F
1	Rate		10%	5%	5%	6%
2	Years		10	20	15	8
3	Principal		$100,000.00	$30,000.00	$80,000.00	$20,000.00
4	Annual Payment					

TEXT FORMATTING

Another type of formatting applies to text. The spreadsheet automatically left-justifies any text that you input. You can also center or right-justify the text if needed. To change the justification of the text within a cell or group of cells, first select the cells and then do the following:

* Click on one of the "Justification" buttons in the toolbar (the icons with lines either left-justified, right justified, or centered).

OR

1. Choose the Format menu. Select the Alignment option in older versions of Excel. In the current Excel version, you will select Cells first and then Alignment.
2. In the Horizontal box, choose a type of justification (Left, Center, Right).
3. Click on the OK button.

To apply this to our example worksheet, suppose we got crazy and wanted to center the words "Rate, Years, and Principal." Select cells A1 through A3. Click on the icon in the toolbar that has centered lines. Voila!

FORMULAS

Formulas can be used to manipulate numeric data. They are entered just as they would be processed algebraically. If the formula is not entered in this manner, an error message will appear. For example, to add the contents of cell A1 to cell A2, the following steps are necessary:

1. In the cell in which you want the result to appear, type: =A1+A2. The equal sign signals to Excel that this is a mathematical expression.
2. Press "Enter" to place the results of the equation in the cell.

The same process applies to subtraction, division, and multiplication. The multiplication symbol is the asterisk (*). The division symbol is the slash (/). Remember to use the equal sign as the beginning character so that the data is identified as a formula. Creating formulas is efficient when you are adding, subtracting, multiplying, or dividing just a few cells; if you wanted to sum a large range of cells, creating a formula would take a long time. This is where special functions are useful.

FUNCTIONS

Functions are basically prewritten formulas. They save time and increase accuracy. To calculate the annual payments for our example worksheet, the use of the @PMT function will be explained below.

1. Click on the cell (C4) in which you want the annual payment to appear.
2. On newer versions of Excel, click on the "fx" icon which represents the Functions Wizard. (Or choose the Insert menu and select the Functions option.) In older versions, choose the Formula menu and select the Paste Functions option.
3. Choose Financial under the Functions category box.
4. Choose PMT under the Function name box. (You may have to click the down arrow until PMT appears on the screen.) Then click Next or OK.
5. Enter the cell locations which contain the rate, nper, and pv. In this example, rate is C1. Nper (years) is C2. Pv (principal) is C3. (The formula is =PMT(rate, nper, pv). Older versions of Excel will also ask for fv and type; delete those. Click on Finish.

Do not yet calculate the remaining annual payments. We will do so using the time-saving copying function in the following section. Exhibit 5.2 includes the annual loan payment calculations.

EXHIBIT 5.2
PAYMENT CALCULATIONS

	A	B	C	D	E	F
1	Rate (Rate)		10%	5%	5%	6%
2	Years (Nper)		10	20	15	8
3	Principal (Pv)		$100,000.00	$30,000.00	$80,000.00	$20,000.00
4	Annual Payment		($16,274.54)	($2,407.28)	($7,707.38)	($3,220.72)

Note: Formula for annual payment in cell C4 is: =PMT(C1,C2,C3).

The spreadsheet program has many useful functions available in addition to those that perform basic arithmetic. Some functions and their symbols are explained in Exhibit 5.3.

EXHIBIT 5.3
USEFUL FUNCTIONS

Financial Functions:

FV	Returns the future value of an investment.
IPMT	Returns the interest payment for an investment for a given period.
IRR	Returns the internal rate of return for a series of cash flows.
NPV	Returns the net present value of an investment based on a series of periodic cash flows and a discount rate.
PMT	Returns period payments for an annuity.
PV	Returns the present value of an investment.
RATE	Returns the interest rate per period of an annuity.

Date and Time Functions:

DATE	Returns the serial number of a particular date.
DAY	Converts a serial number to a particular day of the month.
DAYS360	Calculates the number of days between two dates based on a 360-day year.
TIMEVALUE	Converts the time in the form of text to a serial number.
TODAY	Returns the serial number of today's date.

Math and Trig Functions:

COUNTIF	Returns the number of nonblank cells in a given range which meet the given criteria.
INT	Rounds a number down to the nearest integer.
ROUND	Rounds a number to the specified number of digits.
SUBTOTAL	Returns a subtotal in a list or database.
SUM	Adds the specified numbers.

Statistical Functions:

AVERAGE	Returns the average of the specified numbers
COUNT	Counts how many numbers are in a given range.
MAX	Returns the maximum number in a specified range.
MEDIAN	Returns the median of the specified numbers.
MIN	Returns the minimum number in a specified range.
MODE	Returns the most common value in a specified range.

COPYING

Instead of entering the @PMT function for each loan, you can copy this formula into the other cells. The cell addresses will automatically change as you copy a formula from one cell to another. For example, when copying the cell address for rate in column C onto column D, the address C1 changes to D1 in order to compute the next column of figures. This is referred to as **relative addressing**. This feature enables you to save time and eliminate typing errors when copying or moving data. Copy the formula into the other cells in your worksheet by:

* Using the Copy and Paste buttons. Click on the cell which contains the formula (C4) and click on the Copy button (two pieces of paper). Click on the cell in which you want the formula pasted (D4) and then click on the Paste button (clipboard). Remember, the data stays on the clipboard until you replace it with new data. So, the formula can be pasted into cell E4 by simply clicking on the cell and then clicking on the Paste icon. Repeat with cell F4.

OR

1. Select the cell to be copied, choose the Edit menu and select the Copy option.
2. Select the cell into which you want the function pasted. Press Enter or choose the Edit menu and select the Past option.

The alternative to relative addressing is called **absolute addressing**. This means that the cell references do not adjust, but they remain exactly as they were in the source cell of the copy procedure. To make a formula absolute you must precede that portion of the formula with a dollar sign ($). Thus, if you want to copy a formula such as =C21*D25 and you want to make C21 an absolute address, you would type the formula as =C21*D25 before copying.

Charts/Graphs 6

The spreadsheet program allows you to create charts or graphs as a way to visually represent numeric data. Research has shown that information presented in charts and graphs is often more useful than information shown in tables or columns of numbers alone. Excel refers to both charts and graphs as simply "charts." The following information is based on Excel 97; thus, specific steps may vary slightly with other versions of Excel.

CREATING A CHART

Before creating a chart, you prepare a schedule of the data which is to be graphed. Below is the schedule of data that was used to create the charts on the following pages. Type this data onto an Excel worksheet. Optional: To enhance your worksheet, you can align the regional headings directly above the sales amounts by clicking on the right-justified icon before typing in the heading. Your worksheet should resemble the one below.

	A	B	C	D	E	F
1	SALES BY YEAR AND BY REGION					
2						
3		North	South	East	West	
4	1995	345	518	231	69	
5	1996	218	327	146	44	
6	1997	112	168	75	22	
7	1998	356	534	239	71	
8	1999	178	267	119	36	
9	2000	125	188	84	25	

General instructions will be given to create any chart, and then detailed instructions will be given to create specific charts using the above data.

The first step in creating any chart is to highlight the data on your worksheet which is to be included in the chart. Next, access the Chart Wizard by doing the following:

    *   Click on the Chart Wizard button (icon of a column chart).

OR

    1.   Select "Insert-Chart" from the top menu bar.

The Chart Wizard will guide you through a four step process of creating a chart. The Wizard will present several types of charts from which you can pick. Click on the type you desire and then click "Next." The Wizard will allow you to designate data labels, titles, and legends. Click on "Finish" after making your selections. The chart will appear on your worksheet.

The following sections will describe in more detail how to create specific charts using the example data. To delete a chart from your worksheet, simply click on the chart and press the Delete key.

LINE CHART

A line chart is a standard one-dimensional chart. It is used for plotting data on the vertical y-axis and label data on the horizontal x-axis. The y-axis can contain from one to six ranges, producing one to six lines. Since this information is dependent upon the categories contained on the x-axis, these y-values are known as the dependent variables.

Using the example data, plot a line chart of the North's sales by year. As shown in Exhibit 6.1, the years (the first column of data) is the x-axis and the North's sales (the second column of data) is the y-axis. First, highlight the data needed for the chart: cells B4 thru B9, which contain the North's sales amounts.

Next, click on the Chart Wizard button. The Chart Wizard menu box will appear. In the first step, you must select a specific chart type. Select line chart first, and then you will be able to choose from several chart sub-types. For simplification, we selected the first sub-type choice, "Line," which is described as "Displays trend over time or categories."

Click on "Next." In the second step, you may enter data range and series. The data range was previously highlighted, B4:B9. Select "Series" and in the "Category (x) axis labels" box, click on the right button (diagonal red arrow), then highlight the range containing years 1995 to 2000 (A4 to A9) and press the enter key. Click on "Next" and you will go to Step 3.

In Step 3, you may select chart options, such as titles, legend, and data labels. Select "Legend" and remove checkmark from "show legend" box (simply click on box). Select "Titles" and enter "North Sales by Year" in "Chart Title" box. Click on "Next" and you will go to Step 4.

In Step 4, you will indicate whether to save the chart as a new sheet or object in sheet1. Select the latter so that your chart will be part of sheet1, and thus shown on the worksheet. Click "Finish" and your chart will appear on your worksheet. You can reposition the chart on the worksheet, by clicking on the chart, holding down the left mouse button, and dragging the chart to its new position. Exhibit 6.1 contains an example of a line chart. To print the chart, highlight the chart by clicking on it, then select "Print" or "Print-preview" (viewing prior to printing is usually a good idea). Print-preview allows you to make setup changes such as page orientation (portrait or landscape) and margins, prior to actual printing.

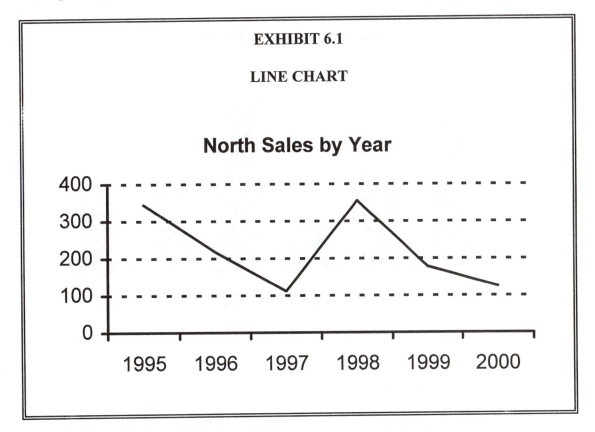

EXHIBIT 6.1

LINE CHART

COLUMN CHART

A column chart, like a line chart, is a one-dimensional chart. You can use Chart Wizard in the same fashion as with the line chart described above. For an example, we will again use the North's sales and chart them by years using columns. The axis remain the same; the years are shown on the x-axis and the sales amounts are shown on the y-axis. Highlight the data needed for the chart: cells B4 through B9.

Next, click on the Chart Wizard button and follow the same instructions as for a line chart except this time you will select the column chart option. Among the chart sub-types of column charts, we selected the first, which is described as "clustered column." As with the previous chart, data is contained in columns. When completed, your column chart should resemble Exhibit 6.2.

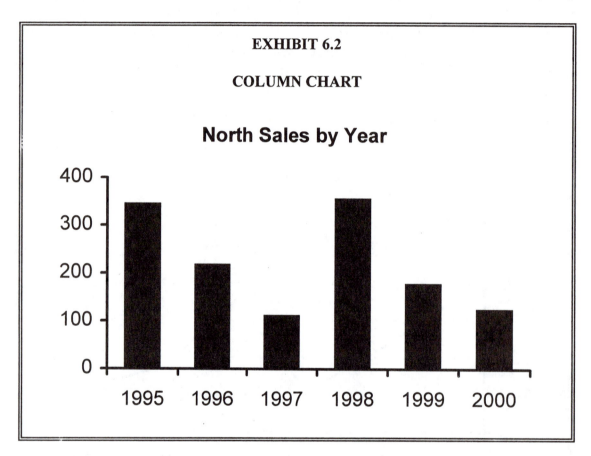

EXHIBIT 6.2

COLUMN CHART

North Sales by Year

STACKED-COLUMN CHART

A stacked-column chart is one variation of a column chart. Instead of placing bars next to each other, it stacks shaded bars for multiple ranges of data on top of each other. This time we will chart the sales for all the geographical regions. Years are listed on the x-axis, sales are the y-axis, and the regions are the different bars in each column.

The data included in the highlighting for this chart are cells B3 through E9. Note that we are including the regional headings in the data-range. Chart Wizard will use these headings for the chart legend, which labels the bars within each column.

Click on the Chart Wizard button and follow the steps previously described. After selecting the column chart type, we chose the second chart sub-type: stacked column.

Your chart should resemble the stacked-column chart of sales according to year and region shown in Exhibit 6.3.

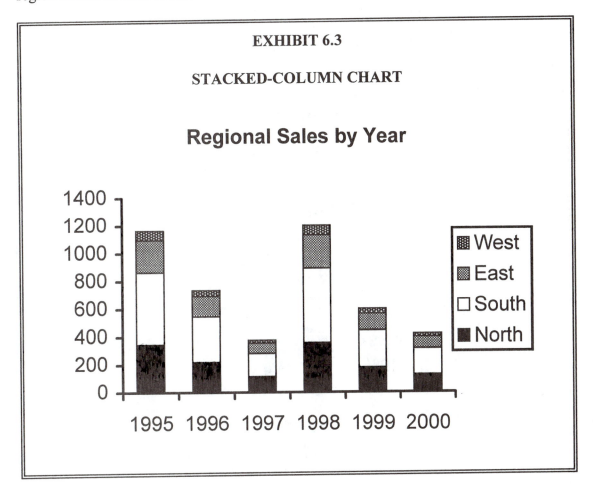

EXHIBIT 6.3

STACKED-COLUMN CHART

Regional Sales by Year

PIE CHART

A pie chart can be used to graph only a single range of data. For example, we will graph each region's sales for the year 1995 only. To do so, highlight cells B3 through E4, which contain the regional names and sales amounts. The regional names will be used as labels for the pie slices.

Click on Chart Wizard and follow the usual steps. In Step 1 we selected "pie" for chart type and for sub-type we selected the first choice which is "pie." Click on "Next" to go to Step 2.

In Step 2, the Excel program automatically identified the data-range we previously highlighted (B3:E4). Click on "Next" to go to Step 3.

Step 3 provides chart options: Titles, Legend, and Data Labels. Select Chart Title and enter: 1995 Sales by Region. Select Legend and remove checkmark from "show legend" box by clicking on box. Select Data Labels and under Data Labels column, select "show label and percent." Click on "Next" to go to Step 4.

In Step 4, click on Place Chart "as object in sheet1." Your pie chart should resemble Exhibit 6.4.

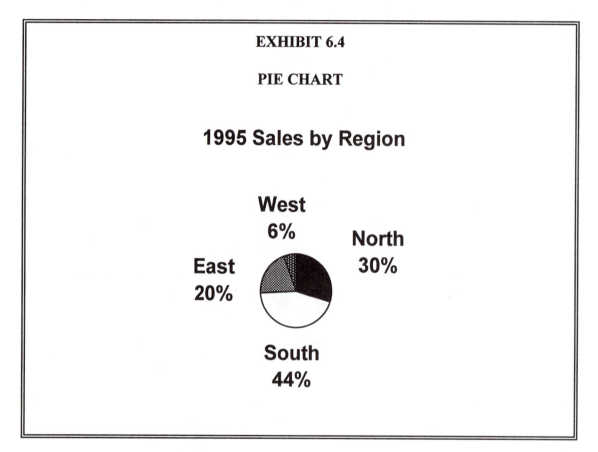

EXHIBIT 6.4

PIE CHART

1995 Sales by Region

Worksheet Manipulation 7

For improved ease in manipulating the data in a worksheet, Excel has several special features. These include naming ranges, freezing panes, splitting the screen, and importing data. Each of these is discussed below.

RANGE NAMES

Using range names is useful in sorting, formatting, copying, and printing. Sometimes keeping track of the cell addresses to be included in a range can be quite tedious. Excel provides a command to name ranges and thus refer to the cell addresses by that name. To create a range name, perform the following:

1. Highlight (paint) the cells that you want to name as a range.
2. Choose the Insert menu and select the Name option.
3. Select the Define option.
4. Type in the name you want for the range. The name can be up to 255 characters.
5. Click on the OK button.

Once the range name has been created, you may use this name anywhere that requires a cell address. The F3 function key can be used to display range names. Simply press F3 and then place the cell pointer on the named range to be used.

This feature is helpful when printing designated portions of a worksheet. For instance, consider the example in Chapter 6 concerning sales by region. Suppose you frequently print a single region's sales and, thus, it would save time to use range names instead of always highlighting the cells. First, name a range (North, South, East, or West) using the steps above. (Note: if you include the title when you initially highlight the range,

Excel will automatically insert the title as the range name.) In order to print a prenamed range, you must first insert the range name in the print area box which is located above cells A and B. Do this by clicking on the down-arrow located above cell B; all the range names will be displayed. Click on the range you want printed and the name will be entered in the box. Then click on the print button.

FREEZE PANES

When working on a large worksheet, sometimes the entire worksheet does not fit on the screen. The Freeze Panes command allows you to freeze rows or columns so that you can see them while you scroll through the entire worksheet. This is especially useful for freezing titles or headings. Exhibit 7.1 illustrates freezing a row containing titles; note that the row numbers along the side skip from "2" to "21".

EXHIBIT 7.1

FREEZE PANES

Microsoft Excel - FREEZE.XLS

File Edit Formula Format Data Options Macro Window Help

Normal

A21   =E$14

	A	B	C	D	E	F	G	H	I
1	AFF	BVF	TPPY	MPPY	APPY	ECP	TFC	TVC	TC
2	---	---	----	----	----	----	---	----	----
21	40	0	0	0	n.a.	n.a.	2000	0	2000
22	10	6	10	1.82	1.67	1.09	2000	600	2600
23	40	11	20	2.22	1.02	1.22	2000	1100	3100
24	40	15	30	2.86	2.00	1.43	2000	1500	3500
25	40	18	40	4.00	2.22	1.80	2000	1800	3800
26	40	20	50	6.67	2.50	2.67	2000	2000	4000
27	40	21	60	6.67	2.86	2.33	2000	2100	4100
28	40	23	70	4.00	3.04	1.31	2000	2300	4300
29	40	26	80	2.86	3.08	0.93	2000	2600	4600
30	40	30	90	2.22	3.00	0.74	2000	3000	5000
31	40	35	100	1.82	2.86	0.64	2000	3500	5500

Ready

The Freeze Panes command allows you to compare any rows or columns of data which are not already adjacent on the worksheet. In older versions of Excel, horizontal and vertical splits are made independently. In newer versions of Excel, horizontal and vertical splits are made simultaneously. To use the Freeze Panes option, perform the following steps:

1.   Position your cell pointer where you want the freeze to be.

   For a **horizontal** freeze, the rows **above** the cell pointer will be frozen. Thus, to freeze the panes as shown in Exhibit 7.1, position your pointer in the first column of row 3. The data above the freeze line will remain stationary, while the data below can be scrolled.

   For a **vertical** freeze, the columns to the **left** of the cell pointer will be frozen. Position your pointer in the top row of the appropriate column. The data to the left of the freeze line will remain stationary, while the data on the right can be scrolled.

2.   Choose the Window menu and select the Freeze Panes option.

In the newer versions of Excel, you can enter the frozen cells by normal manipulation. In the older versions, you can not enter the frozen area. To remove the freeze, choose the Windows menu and select the Unfreeze Panes option.

SPLIT SCREEN

The Split Screen option is similar to freezing panes, it also allows you to see two distant parts of a worksheet by either splitting the screen horizontally or vertically. The difference is that the part of the worksheet chosen to remain constant can also be duplicated on the screen by scrolling past it. Exhibit 7.2 is an example of a vertical split in which you can compare columns which are not adjacent on the worksheet; note that column G is next to column C. The split is after column C; the data to the right side of the split bar can be scrolled. For instance, you can scroll until column M is adjacent to column C.

In older versions of Excel, horizontal and vertical splits are made independently. In newer versions of Excel, horizontal and vertical splits are made simultaneously. To obtain a split screen, perform the following commands:

1.   First, position your cell pointer where you want the split to be.

   A **vertical** split will occur to the **left** of the cell pointer. Thus, for the split shown in Exhibit 7.2, position your pointer in the first row of column D. The data to the left of the split bar will remain stationary while the data on the right can be scrolled.

   A **horizontal** split will occur **above** the cell pointer. Position your

pointer in the first column of the appropriate row. The data above the
split bar will remain stationary while the data below can be scrolled.

2. Choose the Window menu and select the Split option.

OR

*   If your Excel has this option, use the Split Box located above the
    vertical scroll bar or to the right of the horizontal scroll bar. Drag the
    split box down or to the left of the position you want.

Pressing F6 allows you to move back and forth between each side of the split screen.
To remove the splits, double click on the split bars, or choose the Window menu and select
the Remove Split option.

EXHIBIT 7.2

SPLIT SCREEN

Microsoft Excel - SPLIT.XLS

File Edit Formula Format Data Options Macro Window Help

Normal

A21   -E$14

	A	B	C	G	H	I	J	K	I	M
10										
19	AFF	BVF	TPPY	TFC	TVC	TC	ATC	AVC	MC	PY
20	---	---	----	---	----	----	----	----	----	----
21	40	0	0	2000	0	2000	n.a.	n.a.	65	55
22	40	6	10	2000	600	2600	260.0	60.0	55	55
23	40	11	20	2000	1100	3100	155.0	55.0	45	55
24	40	15	30	2000	1500	3500	116.7	50.0	35	55
25	40	18	40	2000	1800	3800	95.0	45.0	25	55
26	40	20	50	2000	2000	4000	80.0	40.0	15	55
27	40	21	60	2000	2100	4100	68.3	35.0	15	55
28	40	23	70	2000	2300	4300	61.4	32.9	25	55
29	40	26	80	2000	2600	4600	57.5	32.5	35	55
30	40	30	90	2000	3000	5000	55.6	33.3	45	55
31	40	35	100	2000	3500	5500	55.0	35.0	55	55
32	40	41	110	2000	4100	6100	55.5	37.3	65	55
33	40	48	110	2000	4800	6800	61.8	43.6	75	55

Ready

IMPORTING DATA

Using the Clipboard feature, you are able to copy or "import" data from other spreadsheets or programs into your Microsoft Excel worksheet. If there is only a portion of data from another spreadsheet or program that you wish to import to your Excel worksheet, then do the following:

1. Open the file which contains the data you want imported into your Excel worksheet.
2. Select the data that you want copied.
3. Choose the Copy option in that program. This allows the data to be copied onto the Clipboard. At this point, you may close the file or leave it open.
4. Next, open the Excel worksheet into which you want to import information.
5. Select the area on the Excel worksheet where the information should be imported.
6. Choose the Edit menu from the Menu Bar.
7. Click on the Paste Special option.

Suppose instead that you have a Lotus 1-2-3 file that you would like to work on in Microsoft Excel or that you want to actually make it a Microsoft Excel file. To import the entire file, start Microsoft Excel and do the following:

1. Choose the File menu from the Menu Bar or click on the Open button in the toolbar.
2. In the List files of Type box, choose the file program that you wish to import from. You can see the different choices by clicking on the down arrow button next to the box. If you do not see the program you want listed, then choose the All Files option.
3. Find the file you wish to import and select it. A box will appear asking you to identify the format you are importing from.
4. Select the program format of the file that you want imported and press the Enter key.

You should note that not every program file type can be imported into Excel. Also, when files such as Lotus 1-2-3 spreadsheets are imported into Microsoft Excel, some changes to the formatting may occur. However, the actual data should import without any changes.

Database Commands *8*

Excel provides a database function which allows you to assimilate and manipulate related information. A database is comprised of **records** which are comprised of **fields.** A field is a single item of data such as an account title, an account number, or amount. Fields that are related are grouped together in records. These records comprise the database. Database input and design follow the same procedures as with the input and design of any worksheet. There are only a few additional functions and commands that are necessary to fully utilize a database.

Exhibit 8.1 displays the worksheet which will be referred to throughout this chapter to illustrate the different commands available.

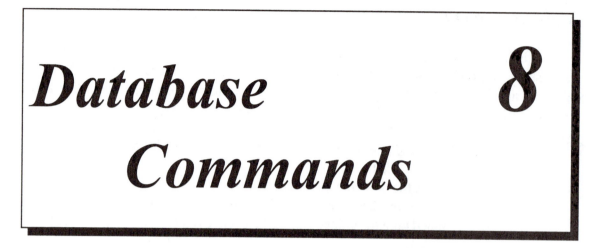

EXHIBIT 8.1

EXAMPLE WORKSHEET

	A	B	C	D
1	ACCOUNT	NAME	BALANCE	PAST DUE
2		JOHN SMITH	220	20
3		SARA JONES	145	40
4		AL JACKSON	50	10
5		AMY BROWN	100	90
6		JAMES KING	200	60
7		ROB MILLER	600	80
8				

DATA FORM

Instead of duplicating the example worksheet by typing data into each cell, you can use an Excel feature called data form. The purpose of data form is to reduce errors resulting from entering data into the wrong cell. When using data form, you provide Excel with the titles you want on the worksheet and it inserts these titles into a simplified form. You can then add information record by record. To duplicate the example worksheet using data form, perform the following steps:

1. Type the titles (i.e., account, name, balance, past due) onto the first row of the worksheet.
2. Highlight the titles with your cell pointer.
3. Select the Data menu and choose the Form option. You will be asked if the top row of your selection is the header row. Click on the OK button.
4. The form will automatically appear with your titles as the field names on the form. You can now begin entering data from your records. IMPORTANT: Use the TAB key when moving from one field to the next. Hit the ENTER key at the end of each record.

When you are finished, your worksheet should resemble Exhibit 8.1.

AUTOFILL

This command enables the user to fill a specified range with a sequence of numbers or text (e.g., 1st quarter). Suppose you want to create a consecutive numbering system for customer account numbers, beginning with account number 1001 up to account number 1006. Perform the following steps:

1. Type in the first two values of the series (i.e., 1001, 1002) in the first two cells of your list. (Refer to Exhibit 8.2.)
2. Highlight the cells in which you just placed your values.
3. In the bottom righthand corner of the cell border you will see a small, darkened box. This box is called the fill handle. Move the cell pointer to the fill handle, and it should turn into a black plus sign (+).
4. Click and drag your mouse (with the +) down over the cells that you want AutoFill to fill in. Release the mouse and AutoFill will fill in the cells that you selected.

The result of this procedure is displayed in Exhibit 8.2.

EXHIBIT 8.2

RESULTS OF AUTOFILL

	A	B	C	D
1	ACCOUNT	NAME	BALANCE	PAST DUE
2	1001	JOHN SMITH	220	20
3	1002	SARA JONES	145	40
4	1003	AL JACKSON	50	10
5	1004	AMY BROWN	100	90
6	1005	JAMES KING	200	60
7	1006	ROB MILLER	600	80
8				

DATA SORT

While designing a worksheet, you may decide to rearrange data within a column. Suppose you want to view the accounts receivable past due from shortest time past due to longest time past due. To perform this sort, execute the following steps:

1. Select the database information that you want to sort. You'll be highlighting each record in its entirety since we want each record to remain intact as it is sorted. Highlight the data below the titles -- NOT the titles.
2. Select the Data menu and choose the Sort option.
3. In the Sort box, select which field to sort by (column D) and whether to sort in ascending or descending order (ascending). Note that you can choose to have three "tiers" of fields to sort by. If there is a tie using your first field, then Excel will sort by the second chosen field.
4. Click on the OK button. Your database should now appear sorted.

The result of Data Sort is shown in Exhibit 8.3. Save this worksheet; it will be used again in Chapter 9.

EXHIBIT 8.3

RESULTS OF DATA SORT

	A	B	C	D
1	ACCOUNT	NAME	BALANCE	PAST DUE
2	1003	AL JACKSON	50	10
3	1001	JOHN SMITH	220	20
4	1002	SARA JONES	145	40
5	1005	JAMES KING	200	60
6	1006	ROB MILLER	600	80
7	1004	AMY BROWN	100	90
8				

AUTOFILTER

This command permits the user to find, select, and delete records in a database according to criteria set forth by the user. You determine your criteria by determining what data from which fields you want to keep. For example, you may choose to see only those records for people who are 40 days or more past due. AutoFilter will allow you to do this by performing the following steps:

1. Highlight all of the records including the titles.
2. Select the Data menu and choose the Filter option and then the AutoFilter.
3. Small boxes with down arrows will appear in each cell containing a field title. These drop boxes will list options when the arrow is clicked.
4. To see the records that are 40 days or more past due, go to the Past Due field title and click on the down arrow. Choose the Custom option within the drop box, since you are customizing your selection.
5. In the Custom AutoFilter menu box, click on the first arrow in order to view your options. Select the >= operator option. Click on the long box next to it and type in **40**. Click the OK button.

Your worksheet should now only display the records that are 40 days or more past due, as shown in Exhibit 8.4. To delete the AutoFilter, once again select Data menu, Filter, and AutoFilter.

EXHIBIT 8.4

RESULTS OF AUTOFILTER

	A	B	C	D
	ACCOUNT	NAME	BALANCE	PAST DUE
1	ACCOUNT	NAME	BALANCE	PAST DUE
2	1002	SARA JONES	145	40
3	1005	JAMES KING	200	60
4	1006	ROB MILLER	600	80
5	1004	AMY BROWN	100	90
6				

Macro Commands 9

Macros are shortcuts which allow you to reduce a series of different commands or keystrokes into a couple of simple clicks of the mouse. Microsoft Excel allows you to "record" the instruction of several commands and then replay or "run" the macro to activate the commands exactly as you performed them. Macros are efficient in performing time-consuming functions which are done frequently.

CREATING A MACRO

To illustrate the macro feature, we will use the example worksheet from Chapter 8. In Chapter 8, the accounts were sorted according to the number of days they were past due. Suppose we want to sort them according to their balance; going from largest to smallest. Since the account balances change often, let's create a macro that runs the sort procedure.

The following steps describe how to create a simple macro, in this case, for sorting a worksheet. First, open the worksheet used in Chapter 8.

1. Turn on the macro recorder by selecting the Tools menu and choosing the Record Macro option and Record New Macro.
2. Enter a name for your macro in the Name box. (You may replace the name Excel automatically inserted with the name "Sort.")
3. Click on the OK button. A small box will appear in the upper righthand of your worksheet labeled "Stop Recording." This means that every action you perform from now until the time you press the button in that box will be recorded.
4. Perform the task you want done. In this case, perform the sort feature: Highlight all the records (but not the titles). The highlighted range

should include cells A2 to D7. Click on the Data menu and choose Sort. In the Sort box, select column C in descending order. Click on OK.

5.   Click on the button in the "Stop Recording" box.

Your worksheet should now resemble Exhibit 9.1.

EXHIBIT 9.1

WORKSHEET SORTED BY BALANCE

	A	B	C	D
	A	B	C	D
1	ACCOUNT	NAME	BALANCE	PAST DUE
2	1006	ROB MILLER	600	80
3	1001	JOHN SMITH	220	20
4	1005	JAMES KING	200	60
5	1002	SARA JONES	145	40
6	1004	AMY BROWN	100	90
7	1003	AL JACKSON	50	10
8				

RUNNING A MACRO

Let's make use of the macro we just created. Suppose the account balances have changed in the past week. John Smith reduced his balance down to $120 and James King reduced his balance down to $80. Insert these new figures into your worksheet. Now we'll resort the accounts using the macro. To run the macro, perform the following steps:

1.   Select the Tools menu and choose the Macro option.
2.   Choose the name macros (i.e., Sort) and click on the Run button.

Your worksheet should now resemble Exhibit 9.2. This sorting task was relatively simple, but it illustrates the potential that macros have in saving time on tasks that must be constantly repeated.

EXHIBIT 9.2

RESULTS OF MACRO

	A	B	C	D
1	ACCOUNT	NAME	BALANCE	PAST DUE
2	1006	ROB MILLER	600	80
3	1002	SARA JONES	145	40
4	1001	JOHN SMITH	120	20
5	1004	AMY BROWN	100	90
6	1005	JAMES KING	80	60
7	1003	AL JACKSON	50	10
8				

Guidelines for **10**
Worksheet Design

The following general guidelines should be considered when designing a worksheet file using Excel or any spreadsheet software:

1. Outline worksheet requirements (i.e., input and output).
2. Create a file identification area.
3. Establish data input areas separate from output areas.
4. Enter data in rows or columns, but not both.
5. Use manual recalculation when working with large files.
6. Create backup files.
7. Test the worksheet.

REQUIREMENTS OUTLINE

The first guideline in creating a worksheet is to outline the worksheet requirements. What input is necessary to solve the problem at hand? What output is required? These requirements should be determined before beginning work. For example, assume that a user is creating a worksheet that projects income statements for the next two years based on a constant growth rate in sales revenue. In addition, cost of goods sold is assumed to be a constant percentage of sales and operating expenses are assumed to be a fixed amount each year. In this case, the following input is required:

a. Current sales amount.
b. Annual sales growth rate.
c. Cost of goods sold as a percentage of sales.
d. Fixed amount of operating expenses.

For purposes of this example, the income statement is limited to only five line items. The output requirement would be projected income statements for the next two years. See Exhibit 10.1 for an illustration.

EXHIBIT 10.1

REQUIRED OUTPUT

	20X1	20X2
Projected Sales	$ XX	$ XX
Cost of Goods Sold	XX	XX
	-------	-------
Gross Profit	XX	XX
Operating Expenses	XX	XX
	-------	-------
Projected Net Income	$ XX	$ XX
	=====	=====

FILE ID

A file identification area should be prepared at the top of the worksheet. This area should include pertinent information such as the file name, the worksheet designer's name, the input required, the output generated, and the dates the file was created, modified, and last used. See Exhibit 10.2 for an illustration.

DATA INPUT AND OUTPUT

Separate areas should be created for input and output in order to facilitate use of the worksheet by users not familiar with it. The input and output areas are illustrated in Exhibit 10.3. The four data items necessary for using the worksheets -- current sales, annual growth rate, cost of goods sold as a percentage of sales, and operating expenses -- are entered in one column of the input area. The output area consists of an income statement with five line items and a separate column for each of the two years projected. Nothing is entered in this area. The output area is totally formula driven based on figures previously entered into the input area.

EXHIBIT 10.2
WORKSHEET IDENTIFICATION AREA

	A	B	C	D	E
1	IDENTIFICATION AREA				
2	--------------------				
3	Filename: Forecast				
4	Designer: Nick Morgan				
5	Input Required:				
6	a. Current Sales Amount				
7	b. Annual Sales Growth Rate				
8	c. Cost of Goods Sold as a % of Sales				
9	d. Operating Expenses				
10	Output: Projected Income Statements				
11	File Created: March 26, 2001				
12	File Modified: June 20, 2001				
13	Last Used: July 20, 2001				

INPUT ALIGNMENT

For maximum efficiency, the input cells should be aligned vertically (in a column) or horizontally (in a row), but not both. Fewer mistakes should occur if the user doesn't have to steer the cursor through a maze of input cells. In Exhibit 10.3 the input area is aligned vertically so that the user can easily move from the first to the last input cell by using the down-arrow key.

MANUAL RECALCULATION

Manual recalculation provides more efficient data entry when working with large worksheets. Usually, the software automatically recalculates mathematical expressions when values are modified or added. Data cannot, however, be entered while the recalculations are taking place. The time involved is inconsequential for small worksheets but can become a burden for large worksheets. A simple procedure is used to change from automatic recalculation to manual recalculation. To do this in Excel, select the Tools menu and choose Options. Select the Calculation sheet. In the Calculation area, choose Manual. Click on OK. After choosing this command, the F9 key must be pressed for recalculation to occur.

EXHIBIT 10.3

INPUT AND OUTPUT AREAS

	A	B	C	D	E
16	INPUT AREA:				
17					
18	Current Sales ($):			1,000	
19	Growth rate as a % of sales:			12%	
20	Cost of goods sold as a % of sales:			60%	
21	Operating Expenses ($):			100	
22					
23					
24	OUTPUT AREA:				
25					
26	PROJECTED INCOME STATEMENT FOR THE NEXT TWO YEARS				
27					
28				20x1	20x2
29				------	------
30	Sales			1120	1254
31	Cost of goods sold			672	753
32				------	------
33	Gross Profit			448	501
34	Operating Expenses			100	100
35				------	------
36	Projected Net Income			348	401
37				======	======
38					
39					
40					

Note: Formulas are as follows:

	20x1	20x2
Sales	=D18+D18*D19	=D30+D30*D19
Cost of Goods Sold	=D30*D20	=E30*D20
Gross Profit	=D30-D31	=E30-E31
Operating Expense	=D21	=D21

BACKUP FILES

Backup copies should be continually updated and stored in more than one place. When creating a worksheet, the user should periodically (every 15 to 30 minutes) save the file in case of a power outage or other event that may cause erasure of the file and the loss of hours of work.

TESTING

Any new worksheet should be manually tested. If formulas are involved, the user must test the worksheet result against an example that is already proven correct.

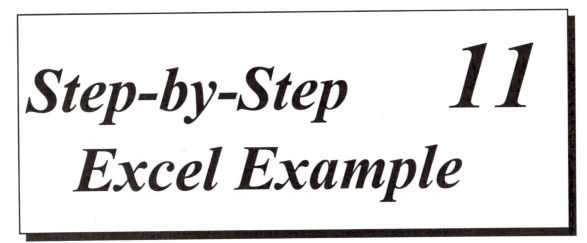

This chapter provides step-by-step instructions for creating a simple worksheet and graph using Microsoft Excel spreadsheet software.

ASSIGNMENT 1: CREATING AN EXCEL WORKSHEET

Type the following income statement into an Excel worksheet. (Note: The sales amount of $1,000 is in cell E5.) If needed, brief reviews of some of the Excel features are given.

	A	B	C	D	E	F
1		JACOB & SISTERS BRICK COMPANY				
2		INCOME STATEMENT				
3		For the Year Ended December 31, 1999				
4						
5	Sales				1000	
6	Cost of sales					
7	Gross profit					
8	Operating expense					
9	Net Income					
10						

Centering. Type the heading into cells A1, A2, and A3. To center the headings, select cells A1 through E3. To select or highlight cells, hold down the left mouse button and drag the curser over the cells you wish to select; the cells will darken. After selecting the cells, click on the framed "a" button in order to center the headings.

Column Expansion. Column A should be expanded to accommodate the long titles. To do so, place the cursor between the column labels A and B until the pointer becomes a black line with arrows on both sides. Hold down the left mouse button and drag the column to the desired width. This will not affect other column widths. The column may be widened after all entries have been made in that column.

Editing a Cell. To change a cell after it has already been entered, return to the edit mode by clicking on the cell and pressing the F2 function key at the top of the keyboard.

Assume that the company expects sales of $1,000 for the year ended 12/31/99. The cost of sales is expected to be 60 percent of sales and operating expenses average 10 percent of sales. Use formulas for all entries except the sales figure (e.g. =E5*.60). Type the following formulas into your worksheet:

	A	B	C	D	E	F
1	JACOB & SISTERS BRICK COMPANY					
2	INCOME STATEMENT					
3	For the Year Ended December 31, 1999					
4						
5	Sales				1000	
6	Cost of sales				=E5*.60	
7	Gross profit				=E5-E6	
8	Operating expense				=E5*.10	
9	Net income				=E7-E8	
10						

Your output (shown on screen) would be as follows:

	A	B	C	D	E	F
1	JACOB & SISTERS BRICK COMPANY					
2	INCOME STATEMENT					
3	For the Year Ended December 31, 1999					
4						
5	Sales				1000	
6	Cost of sales				600	
7	Gross profit				400	
8	Operating expense				100	
9	Net income				300	

Currency Format. If you wish to include dollar signs and commas, click on the cells containing currency. Once the cells are selected, click on the Format menu and choose "Style." To display your options, click on the down arrow next to style name box. Click on Currency (0), which stands for zero decimal places. Then, click on "OK."

Save. When you have finished entering the information and checked the results for accuracy, save your work by clicking on the toolbar "File" and "Save," or clicking on the diskette icon. Remember to save to your directory (e.g., A drive).

Print. Print your income statement using the printer icon. A good suggestion is that you highlight all the information you want printed, then from the menu bar select "File - Print Area - Set Print Area" before clicking on the printer icon. Another very useful step is to select "File - Print Preview" to see how your output will look. By skipping this step, and depending on where the cursor is, you could print several pages unnecessarily.

Open File. Opening a saved worksheet is fairly simple. After starting Excel, click on the folder icon, identify the drive your disk is in, and then double-click on your filename. Once the file is loaded, you may change the sales amount and see how the other values (cost of sales, gross profit, etc.) are automatically updated.

ASSIGNMENT 2: CREATING AN EXCEL PIE CHART

Prepare a pie chart of the division of sales revenue from the data provided in the income statement you prepared above. Skip down a few lines on your worksheet and type in the following schedule of data to be charted:

	A	B	C	D
15	Cost of Sales	600		
16	Op. Expenses	100		
17	Net Income	300		

Select and highlight the data you want charted (i.e., cells A15 through B17). These cells contain Cost of Sales, Op. Expenses, Net Income, and their corresponding dollar amounts. Click on the Chart Wizard button: icon of a bar chart (an alternative to Chart Wizard is to click on the Insert menu and choose "Chart"). The Chart Wizard menu box will appear. In the first step, click on "Pie" for the chart type and then select the chart sub-type. We selected exploded-pie. Then click on "Next" to go to Step 2.

In Step 2, you may designate the data range and series. In the case of this pie chart, nothing needs to be done since we have previously highlighted the data range and series. Click on "Next" to go to Step 3.

In Step 3 you select chart options: data labels, legend, and titles. For data labels, click on "show label and percent." Select "Legend" and remove the legend by clicking on the "show legend" box which contains a checkmark. The click removes the checkmark. Select "Titles" and, under "Chart title," enter PIE GRAPH OF I/S ITEMS. Click on "Next" to go to Step 4.

In Step 4, you indicate whether to save the chart as a new sheet or object in sheet1. Select "object in sheet1." Click on "Finish" and the chart will appear in your worksheet. You can reposition the chart by using the "click and drag" approach previously described in Chapter 6.

When the chart is shown on screen, you can print it just as you would any other document. The chart can be printed as part of the worksheet or separately (simply highlight the chart and select print). The print manager builds the graph slower than ordinary data so expect it to take longer to print.

Your output would appear as shown in Exhibit 11.1 below.

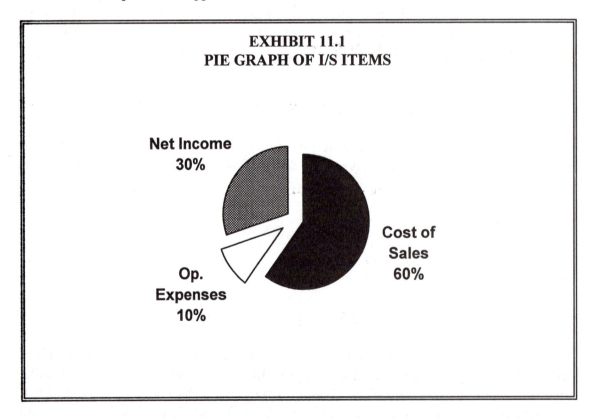

EXHIBIT 11.1
PIE GRAPH OF I/S ITEMS

Net Income 30%

Cost of Sales 60%

Op. Expenses 10%

Spreadsheet Exercises

LIST
of Spreadsheet Exercises

The list below provides a brief description of each exercise and related accounting topic area. Your instructor will designate which exercises you will be assigned to complete. Solutions to odd-numbered exercises 1 to 45 are shown at the end of the book. Also, a number of examples are included on the student disk accompanying this book. **Note**: If the description below includes a number in parentheses, this indicates that the exercise was adapted from Prentice-Hall's *Accounting*, Fourth Edition.

ACCOUNTING TOPIC	EXERCISE No.	DESCRIPTION
1. Accounting and the Business Environment	1	Income Statement
	2	Cost of Goods Sold
	46	Financial Statements (DE 1-10)
	47	Income Statement (DE 1-15)
	48	Statement of Owners Equity (DE 1-16)
2. Recording Business Transactions	3	Double-Entry Accounting
	4	Double-Entry Accounting.
	49	T-Accounts and Trial Balance (E 2-6)
	50	Trial Balance and Income Statement (P 2-5B)
3. Measuring Business Income: The Adjusting Process	51	Preparation of Adjusted Trial Balance (E 3-9)
	52	Financial Statements and Related Questions (P 3-6A)
4. Completing the Accounting Cycle	53	Post Closing Trial Balance (DE4-15)
	54	Trial Balance and Worksheet (E4-1)
5. Merchandising Operations and the Accounting Cycle	25	Sales by Product Type
	55	Balance Sheet (DE 5-16)
	56	Financial Ratios (DE 5-17)

ACCOUNTING TOPIC	EXERCISE No.	DESCRIPTION
18. Financial Statement Analysis	30	Financial Ratios
	31	Financial Ratios
	32	Common Size Balance Sheets
	33	Common Size Balance Sheets
	73	Horizontal Analysis of Income Statement (E 18-2)
19. Management Accounting	74	Cost of Goods Manufactured and Cost of Goods Sold (E 19-6)
	75	Income Statement (E 19-7)
20. Job Costing	76	Work in Progress and Related Questions (E 20-5)
21. Process Costing	77	Compute Equivalent Units -- FIFO (E 21-10)
	78	Compute Equivalent Units -- Weighted Average (E 21-11)
22. Cost-Volume-Profit Analysis and the Contribution Margin Approach to Decision Making	26	Cost-Volume-Profit Analysis
	27	Cost-Volume-Profit Analysis
	28	Cost-Volume-Profit Analysis: Graph
	29	Cost-Volume-Profit Analysis: Graph
	79	Graph Cost Behavior Patterns (E 22-1)
	80	Contribution Margin Income Statement (E 22-2)
23. Master Budget and Responsibility Accounting	81	Departmental Income Statement (E 23-10)
24. Flexible Budgets and Standard Costs	82	Flexible Budget (E 24-1)
	83	Graph Total Lost Line (E 24-2)

1.   INCOME STATEMENT

Create an Income Statement for Chris Ray's Card Shop for year ended 12/31/99. See Chapter 11 for an example. Assume that sales are expected to be $200,000. The cost of sales is 40% of sales and operating expenses are 15% of sales. The income statement should include the following line items: sales, cost of sales, gross profit, operating expenses, and net income.

2.   COST OF GOODS SOLD

Create the following cost of goods sold statement.

DORIS' DIAMOND CO.
COST OF GOODS SOLD
For Year Ended 12/31/99

Beginning Inventory	$100,000
Purchases	50,000
Goods Available	$150,000
Ending Inventory	75,000
Cost of Goods Sold	$ 75,000

3.   DOUBLE-ENTRY ACCOUNTING

Design a worksheet that enables the user to record transactions in general ledger accounts. Additionally, the worksheet should be designed so that the ending balances in the general ledger accounts are used to automatically prepare a trial balance and an income statement.

Use the same approach as shown in the example file, GLEDGER. Starting with a zero balance in all general ledger accounts, enter the following transactions. Print the general ledger.

Jan. 1:	Mary Smith opens a consulting firm with an $8,000 deposit into the firm's checking account.
Jan. 1:	Prepaid three months of rent for $1,500.
Jan. 2:	Borrowed $4,000 with a note payable to purchase a computer with a two-year useful life and a salvage value of $400.
Jan. 3:	Purchased office supplies on credit for $800.
Jan. 10:	Provided consulting services on account for $3,200.
Jan. 12:	Provided consulting services on account for $1,200.
Jan. 15:	Received partial payment of $1,600 for services rendered on account on January 10.
Jan. 20:	Provided consulting services on account for $2,000.
Jan. 25:	Paid telephone bill of $375.
Jan. 26:	Paid electric bill of $225.
Jan. 31:	Make adjusting entry to record expiration of one month of prepaid rent.
Jan. 31:	Make adjusting entry to record use of office supplies. One-half of supplies have been used.
Jan. 31:	Record depreciation on office equipment for one month. Use straight-line depreciation.
Jan. 31:	The owner, Mary Smith, withdraws $4,000 for personal use.

4.   DOUBLE-ENTRY ACCOUNTING

Using information from the prior exercise, print the trial balance and income statement.

5.   COST OF MERCHANDISE

Design a worksheet which will compute the cost of merchandise purchased. The worksheet should show the cost with and without the discount. The discount should be shown as the difference between these two amounts. Assume that you have purchased merchandise with a gross price of $5,000. This merchandise is subject to a trade discount of 30%. The trade discount is subtracted from the gross price to determine your actual purchase price. The credit terms offered to your company are 2/10 net 30. What is the amount due assuming that you do not take advantage of the discount period? What do you owe if you do take advantage of the discount?

6.   COST OF MERCHANDISE

Same as above but you purchased $10,000 worth of merchandise rather than $5,000.

7.   TRACKING INVENTORY QUANTITY

Design a worksheet which will enable you to enter inventory data. The information should include an item number, description, quantity on hand, and quantity desired. The worksheet should then calculate the amount by which the quantity on hand is above or below the desired quantity by use of a formula. Use the following information to complete the worksheet:

Item No	Description	Quantity on hand	Quantity desired
100	HAMMER	8	30
200	SCREWDRIVER	26	20
300	SAW	57	45
400	WRENCH	34	20
500	PLIERS	5	15

8.   PRODUCT COST SCHEDULE

Prepare a cost schedule for Product X and Product Y using the following layout:

(Input Area)	Product X	Product Y
Total Units		
DM Cost/Unit		
DL Cost/Unit		
OH allocation rate		
Total OH (X & Y)		

(Output Area)

Company Name
Product Cost Schedule
Date

	Product X	Product Y
Direct Materials		
Direct Labor		
Manufacturing Overhead		
Total Cost		

The costs of the direct material for the two products are $2.00 per unit for X and $3.00 per unit for Y. The direct labor costs are $.25 per unit produced for either product. The total manufacturing overhead for the year is $300,000. This should be allocated to the different products based on the ratio of each product's production to total production. Austin company produced 100,000 units of product X and 50,000 units of product Y.

9. STRAIGHT-LINE DEPRECIATION

Design a worksheet that will enable you to compute the annual depreciation expense of a fixed asset using the straight-line method. Assume ABC company bought a machine on July 1 of this year for $20,000. ABC expects the machine to have a useful life of ten years and a $2,000 salvage value at the end of that time. Calculate depreciation expense for this machine in the current year assuming a December 31 year-end.

10. STRAIGHT-LINE DEPRECIATION

Same as above but the salvage value is changed from $2,000 to $4,000; and the machine was purchased on October 1 rather than July 1.

11. SUM-OF-THE-YEARS-DIGITS DEPRECIATION

Design a worksheet which will allow you to calculate the sum-of-the-years-digits depreciation on equipment for the current year. Assume that you bought a machine on January 1 of Year 1 for $250,000. It is expected to have a $24,000 salvage value. Its useful life is estimated to be 10 years. You are completing the financial statements for the year ended December 31, Year 4. What is the SYD depreciation that should be included as an expense for Year 4? The following formula can be used to compute SYD Depreciation: =SYD(COST,SALVAGE,LIFE,PERIOD).

12. UNITS-OF-PRODUCTION DEPRECIATION

Create a worksheet which will calculate deprecation on a machine based on the units-of-production method of depreciation. Assume that you bought a machine on January 1 of Year 1 for $150,000. It has a $2,000 salvage value and a useful life of 100,000 units. Calculate the depreciation expense, accumulated depreciation, and net machine (cost less accumulated depreciation) that would be shown on the balance sheet for the first three years of use based on the following information:

UNITS PRODUCED

1ST year	15,000
2ND year	20,000
3RD year	18,000

13.   BAD DEBT EXPENSE

Use the following information to calculate bad debt expense for 1999:

Age of Accounts	A/R Balance	Percent Uncollectible
Under 30 days	$45,000	1%
31-60 days	25,000	3%
61-120 days	15,000	10%
Over 120 days	10,000	30%
Total	$95,000	

Prepare a worksheet demonstrating your computations.

14.   BAD DEBT EXPENSE

Now, assume that bad debt expense is 1% of credit sales. Using the following information, calculate bad debt expense for 1999:

Sales during 1999:

Cash Sales	$100,000
Credit Sales	200,000
Total Sales	$300,000

15.   CASH BUDGET

Create a spreadsheet file of the following cash budget:

	MARCH	APRIL
Cash balance, beginning	$10,000	$29,500
Cash collections from customers	25,000	15,000
Sale of an asset	12,000	0
Total Available	$47,000	$44,500

Cash disbursements:

Purchases	$12,000	$ 8,000
Operating expenses	5,500	2,225
Total Disbursements	$17,500	$10,225
Cash balance, ending	$29,500	$34,275

16.   CASH BUDGET

Refer to the exercise above, but assume that the beginning cash balance on March 1 is now $15,000 and purchases are $10,000 (not $8,000) in April. Recompute the cash budget.

17.   INTEREST EARNED

Design a worksheet which will enable you to compute the interest earned on a note. The input area should include the following items:

    Principal amount of the note
    Interest rate
    Length of time the note has been held (# of days)

The output area of the worksheet should calculate the interest earned using the items in the input area. Assume that you purchased a note on November 1 of this year with a principal amount of $1,000. Assume further that the amount you paid equalled the face amount of the note and the annual interest rate is 7 percent. How much interest earned should you report at December 31 of this year assuming that you do not sell the note before the end of the year?

18.   FUTURE VALUE OF A SINGLE DEPOSIT

Create a worksheet which will enable you to compute the length of time required for a lump sum investment made today to grow to a desired future value. For this exercise, assume that you have $40,000 to invest today and that the investment will always earn an 8 percent return. How long must you leave the money in the account before your investment is worth $500,000? Use the following formula:
    =NPER(Interest Rate,,-Present Value,Future Value).

19.   WEIGHTED AVERAGE NUMBER OF SHARES OF STOCK

Design a worksheet which will enable you to compute the weighted average number of shares of common stock outstanding during the year. In January, there are 500 shares of common stock outstanding. In April, the company sold 700 additional shares. In August, the company purchased 200 of its shares. In September, it issued 800 shares. In November it bought back 300, and in December it sold 500. Assume that all transactions took place on the first day of the month in which they occurred. If today is December 31, what was the weighted average number of shares outstanding during the year?

20.   JOINT COST ALLOCATION

You are performing an audit on a small company and must ensure that the total joint costs are allocated correctly among the three products of the company. Use the following information to compute the cost allocated to each product.

NOTE: Total costs to be allocated are $450,000.

Product	Sales Value at Split-Off
A	$500,000
B	300,000
C	200,000

Prepare a worksheet demonstrating your computations.

21.   JOINT COST ALLOCATION

Referring to the prior exercise, calculate the joint costs to be allocated to the three products assuming that total costs are $600,000 and the sales values at split-Off are as follows:

Product	Sales Value at Split-off
A	$800,000
B	500,000
C	700,000

22.   AGING SALES INVOICES

Design a worksheet which will enable the user to enter information from uncollected sales invoices. The information should include invoice number, date, amount, firm, and term. The worksheet should be able to calculate the number of days past due for each invoice (account receivable). It should also produce an aging schedule based on days past due. You need to include a line for the current date on the worksheet. You can use the command "=today( )" to make this always show the actual date, but it might be more interesting to set it up so that it can be changed manually. Thus, you can experiment with different dates to see what happens with the aging analysis. For this exercise, use 11/15/99 as the current date. Enter the date as "=date(99,11,15)" and then use Format-Cells-Number-Date to display the date in the customary way.

A simple formula should be used to find the number of days outstanding for each receivable. To do this, simply subtract the sales invoice date from the current date shown on the worksheet. This will indicate the number of days that have elapsed since the invoice date; then subtract this number from the number of days in the term (e.g. 30 or 60, as in n/30 or n/60). The result is the number of days past due. Last, sort the invoices by days past due.

Use the following layout for the output area: Current Date: 11/15/99

A	B	C	D	E F G H	I	J
					DAYS	DAYS
UNCOLLECTED						
INVOICE	DATE	AMOUNT	FIRM	TERMS	O/S	PAST DUE
300	08/25/99	$950	BLUE	1 10 N 60	82	22

The input area should include the following uncollected invoices:

INVOICE #	DATE	AMOUNT	FIRM	TERMS
225	05/25/99	$950	BLUE	1 10 N 60
301	06/17/99	235	RED	2 10 N 60
302	07/02/99	340	RED	2 10 N 60
303	07/03/99	560	BLUE	1 10 N 60
307	08/18/99	270	PINK	N 60
309	09/15/99	880	PINK	N 30
312	09/22/99	1690	BLUE	1 10 N 60
317	10/02/99	120	PINK	N 30
318	10/03/99	490	PINK	N 30
319	10/07/99	460	BLUE	1 10 N 60

23. AGING SALES INVOICES

Same assignment as the prior exercise, but in the output area, add a row at the bottom showing average days for term, days outstanding, and days past due.

24. AGING SALES INVOICES

Using the worksheet created in the prior exercise, change the current date to October 1, 1999. Print the revised aging schedule.

25. SALES BY PRODUCT TYPE

Using the data below in the input area, prepare a new report sorted by current-month sales.

SALES SUMMARY REPORT BY PRODUCT TYPE
February

Product Type	Current Month Sales	Prior Month Sales	% Chg.	Year to Date Sales	Last Yr. YTD Sales	% Chg.
A	16	25	-36%	80	100	-20%
B	52	45	16%	260	234	11%
C	44	32	38%	220	154	43%
D	72	67	7%	360	333	8%
E	35	37	-5%	175	180	-3%

26. COST-VOLUME-PROFIT ANALYSIS

Prepare a worksheet that illustrates cost-volume-profit (CVP) analysis, also referred to as break-even analysis. Use the following formulas:

CMU = SPU - VCU
   Where: CMU is contribution margin per unit.
          SPU is sales price per unit.
          VCU is variable cost per unit.

BEP (units) = TFC / CMU
Where: TFC is total fixed cost.
         CMU is contribution margin per unit.

Assume that sales price per unit is $10; that variable cost per unit is $8; and that total fixed cost is $24,000. Calculate the contribution margin per unit, the break-even point in units of sales, and the break-even point in dollars of sales.

27.   COST-VOLUME-PROFIT ANALYSIS

Same as above but the sales price per unit is increased from $10 to $12.

28.   COST-VOLUME-PROFIT ANALYSIS: GRAPH

Assume that sales price per unit is $12, variable cost per unit is $8, and total fixed cost is $24,000. Prepare a graph to illustrate break-even analysis. Hint: Set up a column for units (zero to 8,000 in increments of 1,000), total fixed cost, total variable cost, total cost, sales revenue, and profit. Use this data to prepare the graph. The x-range would be the column showing units, the a-range would be the column showing total fixed cost, etc.

29.   COST-VOLUME-PROFIT ANALYSIS: GRAPH

Same as above, but change total fixed cost from $24,000 to $10,000.

30.   FINANCIAL RATIOS

Use the following formulas to compute financial ratios for Junior's Computer Store for 19x4. The balance sheet and income statement for 19x4 and 19x3 are provided below. Design the worksheet so that the financial statements are in the input area and the financial ratios are in the output area.

FINANCIAL RATIOS:

Liquidity Ratios:
     Current Ratio =   (Cur. Assets)/(Cur. Liabilities)
     Acid-Test Ratio =   (Cur. Assets - Inven. - Prepaid Exp.)/(Cur. Liabilities)

Activity Ratios:

Receivables Turnover =	(Net Credit Sales)/(Avg. A/R)
Inventory Turnover =	(Cost of Goods Sold)/(Avg. Inventory)
Asset Turnover =	(Net Sales)/(Avg. Assets)

Profitability Ratios:

Earnings Per Share =	(Net Inc. - Pref. Div.)/(Common Shares Outstanding)
Price to Earnings (P/E) =	(Market Price per Com. Share)/(EPS)
Dividend Payout =	(Div. per Com. Share)/(EPS)
Sales Profit Margin =	(Net Income)/(Net Sales)
Return on Assets =	(Net Income + Int. Exp. - Tax Savings from Int. Exp.)/(Avg. Assets)
Return on Com Stk Equity =	(Net Inc. - Pref. Div.)/(Avg. Com. Stk Equity)

Financial Stability Ratios:

Total Debt to Total Assets =	(Total Liabilities)/(Total Assets)
Times Interest Earned =	(Earnings before Int. and Taxes)/(Interest Charges)
Book Value Per Share =	(Com. Stk Equity)/(Com. Shares Out.)
Cash Flow Per Share =	(Net Income + Noncash Charges)/(Com. Shares Outstanding)

FINANCIAL STATEMENTS:

Junior's Computer Store
Comparative Balance Sheets
12/31/x4 and 12/31/x3

	12/31/x4	12/31/x3
ASSETS:		
Cash	$1,200,000	$ 1,100,000
Accounts Receivable	780,000	550,000
Inventory	1,850,000	1,600,000
Fixed Assets (net)	8,200,000	7,200,000
Total Assets	$12,030,000	$10,450,000
LIABILITIES:		
Accounts Payable	$1,200,000	$900,000
Long-Term Debt	1,730,000	430,000
Total Liabilities	$2,930,000	$1,330,000
STOCKHOLDERS EQUITY:		
Preferred stock, $100 par, 12% cum	$1,800,000	$1,800,000
Common stock, $100 par	7,000,000	7,000,000
Retained Earnings	300,000	320,000
Total	$9,100,000	$9,120,000
Total Liabilities + Stockholders Equity	$12,030,000	$10,450,000
Market Price of Common Stock	$109	$107

Junior's Computer Store
Comparative Income Statements
FYE 12/31/x4 and 12/31/x3

	12/31/x4	12/31/x3
Sales	$4,000,000	$3,300,000
Cost of Goods Sold	2,200,000	1,650,000
Gross Profit	$1,800,000	$1,650,000
Operating Expenses:		
Depreciation	$738,000	$576,000
Advertising	45,000	38,000
Other	120,000	140,000
Total Operating Expense	$903,000	$754,000
Operating Income	$897,000	$896,000
Interest on Long-Term Debt	80,000	80,000
Income Before Taxes	$817,000	$816,000
Taxes	326,800	326,400
Net Income	$490,200	$489,600
Dividends Declared on Preferred Stock	$220,000	$220,000
Dividends on Common Stock	290,200	299,600
Net Income to Retained Earnings	($20,000)	($30,000)

NOTE: All sales are credit sales; the tax rate is 40%.

31.   FINANCIAL RATIOS

Same as above but change the following 19x4 items:
   (a) Accounts Receivable: $780,000 to $1,780,000
   (b) Accounts Payable: $1,200,000 to $1,400,000
   (c) Retained Earnings: $300,000 to $1,100,000
   (d) Sales: $4,000,000 to $5,000,000
NOTE: The change in these financial statement items will affect other items.

32. COMMON-SIZE BALANCE SHEETS

Using the comparative balance sheets in Exercise 30, prepare common-size balance sheets. To prepare common-size balance sheets, divide all items by the "total assets" amount; thus, total assets each year (i.e., 19x4 and 19x3) will be shown as 100 percent.

33. COMMON-SIZE BALANCE SHEETS

Using the revisions to the 19x4 balance sheet given in Exercise 31, prepare common-size balance sheets for 19x4 and 19x3.

Background for exercises 34 to 39: FOREIGN CURRENCY TRANSLATION

When a multinational corporation based in the U.S. owns more than 50 percent of the voting stock of a foreign company, a parent-subsidiary relationship exists. The parent company is usually required to prepare consolidated financial statements. Before this can be done, the financial statements of the foreign subsidiary must be recast using U.S. generally accepted accounting principles (GAAP). Next, the foreign accounts must be remeasured (translated) from the foreign currency into U.S. dollars. To make the translation, the first step is to identify three currencies: (a) currency of books and records (CBR) -- the CBR is the currency in which the foreign financial statements are denominated; (b) functional currency (FC) -- the FC is the one in which the subsidiary generally buys, sells, borrows, repays, etc.; and (c) the reporting currency (RC) -- the RC is the one in which the consolidated financial statements are denominated. There are basically three approaches to currency translation: (1) temporal rate method, (2) current rate method, and (3) use of both methods. The following three rules are used to determine the method of translation:

Rule 1: If the FC is hyper-inflationary (i.e., 100% cumulative inflation within three years), then ignore the FC and remeasure the CBR into the RC using the temporal rate method.

Rule 2: If the CBR is different from the FC, then remeasure the CBR into the FC using the temporal rate method.

Rule 3: Translate from the FC into the RC using the current rate method.

You must apply the rules in sequence, stopping when the subsidiary's financial statements have been converted into the parent's reporting currency (RC). For example, when the functional currency (FC) is hyper-inflationary, then Rule 1 applies; that is, the financial statements which are denominated in the CBR are translated into the RC using the temporal rate method, and Rules 2 and 3 aren't used. A second example is as follows: If the CBR is British pounds, the FC is Dutch guilders (not hyper-inflationary), and the RC is U.S. dollars; then you skip Rule 1 and apply Rule 2, translating the CBR (pounds) into the FC (guilders) using the temporal rate method. Since the FC (guilders) is not the RC (dollars), you would then apply Rule 3 to translate the FC (guilders) into the RC (dollars) using the current rate method. A third example is as follows: When the CBR is the same as the FC, then you go directly to Rule 3.

Using the current rate method, all assets and liabilities are translated using the current rate (i.e., exchange rate on the balance sheet date). Owners' equity and dividends are translated at historical rates (exchange rate at the time the asset was acquired, liability incurred, or element of paid-in capital was issued or reacquired). Income statement items can be translated using the average exchange rate (the average of the exchange rate at the beginning of the accounting period and the current rate).

Under the temporal rate method, the objective is to measure each subsidiary transaction as though the transaction had been made by the parent. Monetary items (e.g. cash, receivables, inventories carried at market, payables, and long-term debt) are remeasured using the current exchange rate. Other items (e.g. prepaid expenses, inventories carried at cost, fixed assets, and stock) are remeasured using historical exchange rates.

34.   FOREIGN CURRENCY TRANSLATION USING THE CURRENT RATE METHOD

First, read the background information for this problem on the preceding page. Translate the following account balances from Dutch guilders to U.S. dollars using the current rate method.

Adjusted Trial Balance
In Dutch Guilders (DG)
December 31, Year 4

	Debit	Credit
Cash	20,000	
Accounts Receivable	35,000	
Inventory	105,000	
Equipment	60,000	
Accum. Dep.		20,000
Accounts Payable		35,000
Bonds Payable		50,000
Revenues		120,000

General Expenses	108,000	
Depreciation Expense	8,000	
Dividends	4,000	
Common Stock		62,000
Paid-in Capital in Excess of Par		44,000
Retained Earnings		9,000
Total	340,000	340,000

Exchange Rates:

	1 DG = $___
Current Exchange Rate	0.520
Average Exchange Rate	0.490
At July 31, Year 4	0.505
At June 30, Year 1	0.470

Other: All common stock was issued on June 30, Year 1 (i.e., 6/30/Y1).
            Dividends were declared and paid on July 31, Year 4.
            Translated Retained Earnings at 12/31/Y3 was: $5,500.

35.   FOREIGN CURRENCY TRANSLATION USING THE CURRENT RATE METHOD

Same as previous exercise, except the exchange rates are as follows:

Current Exchange Rate	1.200
Average Exchange Rate	1.250
At July 31, Year 4	1.300
At June 30, Year 1	1.000

36.   FOREIGN CURRENCY TRANSLATION USING THE CURRENT RATE METHOD

Use the following information to translate from British pounds to U.S. dollars using the current rate method. Background information is on page 76.

Adjusted Trial Balance
In British Pounds
December 31, Year 8

	Debit	Credit
Cash	72,000	
Accounts Receivable	60,000	
Inventory	136,000	
Fixed Assets	130,000	
Accum. Dep.		76,000
Accounts Payable		50,000
Bonds Payable		90,000
Revenues		172,000
General Expenses	158,000	
Depreciation Expense	10,000	
Dividends	4,000	
Common Stock		58,000
Paid-in Capital in Excess of Par		98,000
Retained Earnings		26,000
Total	570,000	570,000

Exchange Rates:

	1 BP = $___
Current Exchange Rate	2.100
Average Exchange Rate	2.000
At July 31, Year 8	2.050
At June 30, Year 1	1.500

Other:

All common stock was issued on June 30, Year 1 (i.e., 6/30/Y1).

Dividends were declared and paid on July 31, Year 8.

Translated Retained Earnings at 12/31/Y7 was $22,600.

37. FOREIGN CURRENCY TRANSLATION USING THE CURRENT RATE METHOD

Same as previous exercise, except use the following exchange rates:

Current Exchange Rate	3.100
Average Exchange Rate	2.900
At July 31, Year 8	2.950
At June 30, Year 1	4.000

38.   FOREIGN CURRENCY TRANSLATION USING THE TEMPORAL RATE METHOD

Use the temporal rate method to remeasure from the currency of books and records (i.e., British pounds) to the functional currency (i.e., U.S. dollars).

Adjusted Trial Balance
In British Pounds
December 31, Year 4

	Debit	Credit
Cash	52,000	
Accounts Receivable	60,000	
Inventory		
(10-31-Y3)	40,000	
(7-31-Y4)	160,000	
Fixed Assets		
(6-30-Y1)	13,000	
(12-31-Y1)	65,000	
(7-31-Y2)	52,000	
Accum. Dep.		
(6-30-Y1)		8,000
(12-31-Y1)		40,000
(7-31-Y2)		32,000
Accounts Payable		43,000
Bonds Payable		160,000
Revenues		214,000
General Expenses	189,000	
Depreciation Expense		
(6-30-Y1)	1,500	
(12-31-Y1)	7,500	
(7-31-Y2)	6,000	
Dividends (7-31-Y4)	10,000	
Common Stock		
(6-30-Y1)		48,000
(1-31-Y2)		32,000
Paid-in Capital in Excess of Par		
(6-30-Y1)		30,000
(1-31-Y2)		20,000
Retained Earnings		29,000
Total	656,000	656,000

Exchange Rates:

	1 BP = $___
Current Exchange Rate	0.600
Average Exchange Rate	0.610
At July 31, Year 4	0.606
At October 31, Year 3	0.591
At July 31, Year 2	0.585
At January 31, Year 2	0.586
At December 31, Year 1	0.590
At June 30, Year 1	0.580

Other:

Regarding common stock, 60% was issued 6/30/Y1; 40% on 1/31/Y2.

Regarding inventory, 20% was acquired 10/31/Y3; 80% on 7/31/Y4.

Dividends were declared and paid on 7/31/Y4.

Regarding fixed assets, 10% were acquired 6/30/Y1; 50% on 12/31/Y1; and 40% on 7/31/Y2.

Revenues and expenses were accrued evenly throughout the year.

Translated retained earnings at 12/31/Y3 was $16,400

39. FOREIGN CURRENCY TRANSLATION USING THE TEMPORAL RATE METHOD

Same as previous exercise, except use the following exchange rates:

	1 BP = $___
Current Exchange Rate	2.000
Average Exchange Rate	2.400
At July 31, Year 4	2.300
At October 31, Year 3	2.150
At July 31, Year 2	2.200
At January 31, Year 2	2.180
At December 31, Year 1	2.250
At June 30, Year 1	2.100

Background for Exercises 40 to 44: Comparative Advantage

Productivity provides an economic basis for trade. During the early 1800s, David
Ricardo and other economists provided an explanation for trade based on different levels
of productivity among nations in different industries. This can be illustrated as follows.
First, assume that there is only one factor of production, labor. Next, assume that a
worker in the country of Bigred can produce either 8 bales of cotton or 4 crates of apples,
and that a worker in the country of Bigblue can produce either 1 bale of cotton or 1 crate
of apples. Table A shows production in Bigred and Bigblue.

Table A
Cotton and Apples as Produced by Bigred and Bigblue

	Bigred Worker	Bigblue Worker
Cotton	8 bales	1 bale
Apples	4 crates	1 crate

Opportunity costs of production are shown in Table B below.

Table B
Opportunity Costs of Production in Bigred and Bigblue

Bigred:	8 bales of cotton cost 4 crates of apples, so
	1 bale of cotton costs 1/2 crate of apples.
	4 crates of apples cost 8 bales of cotton, so
	1 crate of apples costs 2 bales of cotton.
Bigblue:	1 bale of cotton costs 1 crate of apples.
	1 crate of apples costs 1 bale of cotton.

Table A shows that a worker in Bigred is more productive in both cotton and apples than
a worker in Bigblue. The Bigred worker has an "absolute advantage" in productivity in
both industries. When industries are compared, the Bigred worker is found to be
relatively more productive in the cotton industry (8 to 1) than in the apple industry (4 to
1) in relation to the Bigblue worker. Thus, the Bigred worker has a "comparative
advantage" in the cotton industry. Thus, Bigred's absolute advantage in cotton is
proportionately greater than its absolute advantage in apples.

A lower skilled and lower productive nation will have a comparative advantage in something because there will be some industry in which it is least disadvantaged. If Bigred is better at producing apples than Bigblue, why won't Bigred produce its own apples? The answer is that Bigred determines it more advantageous to produce what it does best, cotton, and trading this cotton for apples. Table C, which is derived from Table B, shows what prices would have to be in effect for trade to be beneficial.

Table C
Prices at Which Trade Would Occur

Bigred: If 1 bale of cotton sells for more than 1/2 crate of apples, Bigred gains by selling cotton.

               If 1 crate of apples sells for less than 2 bales of cotton, Bigred gains by buying apples.

Bigblue: If 1 bale of cotton sells for less than 1 crate of apples, Bigblue gains by buying cotton.

               If 1 crate of apples sells for more than 1 bale of cotton, Bigblue gains by selling apples.

Thus: If the price of apples on the world markets is between 1 bale of cotton and 2 bales of cotton, and if the price of apples is between 1/2 crate of apples and 1 crate of apples, trade is mutually advantageous.

Table D shows the change in world output if firms in each nation reallocate workers to the industry in which the nation has a comparative advantage. The Bigred cotton industry hires a worker away away from the apple industry, and the Bigblue apple industry hires five workers away from the cotton industry. Consequently, the world output of cotton increases by 3 bales, and the world output of apples increases by 1 crate.

Table D
Increase in World Production Based on Transfers of
One Worker in Bigred and Five Workers in Bigblue

	One Bigred Worker	Five Bigblue Workers	World Output
Cotton (bales)	+1	-5	+3
Apples (crates)	-1	+5	+1

Assume that the Bigred firm exports 4 bales of cotton to Bigblue, and that the price of a bale of cotton is 0.7 crates of apples. The trade yields Bigred 2.8 crates of apples. Before international trade, the Bigred firm could have obtained only 2 crates of apples for its 4 bales of cotton. Before international trade, the Bigblue could have obtained only 2.8 bales of cotton for its 2.8 crates of apples, but now gets 4 bales of cotton for its 2.8 crates. The price determines which country receives the greatest benefit. For example, if 1 bale of cotton equals to 0.8 crates of apples, Bigred would have benefitted more from the trade than where the price was 0.7 crates. However, as long at the price falls within the range shown in Table C, both countries gain from specialization and trade. If the costs of production of cotton and apples remained constant, eventually all cotton would be produced in Bigred and all apples in Bigblue. However, increasing costs will probably occur at some point; the cost of producing cotton in Bigred will increase, and the cost of producing apples in Bigblue will increase. At this point, trade is curtailed. Consequently, it is rarely the case that one country produces all of one product.

Effects of an Import Quota

Given the above presentation of comparative advantage, you can understand why the great majority of economists strongly support free trade and oppose the use of tariffs and quotas that impede the free exchange of goods and services. However, there are political motivations that advocate protection of domestic industry. The political motivations for advocating protectionism generally are not supported by sound economic analysis.

40.   ECONOMIC IMPACT OF AN IMPORT QUOTA

First, read the background information for this problem on page 82.
Use the following equation to prepare a domestic demand curve:
$$P(QD) = 100 - 10 * Q$$

Use the following equations to prepare a domestic supply and a world supply curve:
$$P(QS\text{-}d) = 0 + 10 * Q$$
$$P(QS\text{-}w) = 20 + 0*Q$$

The demand curve represents the home country's demand for a homogeneous good (e.g. corn, iron, rubber, etc.). The domestic supply curve is a typical upward-sloping curve. The world market price is $20; thus, persons may import as much as they want at a constant price of $20. In other words, the world supply curve is perfectly elastic at a price of $20. Assume that an import quota of 4 units is established.

Prepare the following:
a.   Table of Q (from 0 to 10, in increments of 1), P(QD), P(QS-domestic), and
       P(QS-world).

b.   Graph the domestic demand curve (P(QD), domestic supply curve (P(QS-d), world supply curve (P(QS-w), and a vertical line at the quantity of 4 to illustrate the effect of the quota.

c.   What is equilibrium price and quantity before and after the quota?

d.   Who are the winners and losers from the quota?

41.   ECONOMIC IMPACT OF AN IMPORT QUOTA

Same as previous exercise, except for the following changes:

    1. The demand equation is as follows: P(QD) = 120 - 10*Q

    2. The world market price is $30.

    3. The domestic supply and world supply equations are as follows:

        P(QS-d) = 20 + 10*Q

        P(QS-w) = 30 + 0*Q

    4. The quota is set at 3 units.

42.   ECONOMIC IMPACT OF A TARIFF

Background information for this problem is on page 82.

Use the following information and analyze the impact of a tariff. Use the following equation to prepare a domestic demand curve:

    P(QD) = 120 - 1*Q

Use the following equations to prepare a supply curve before and after the tariff is implemented. The tariff is set at $20.

    P(QS) = 20 + 1*Q

    P(QS)+T = (20 + 1*Q) + T

Prepare the following:

a.   Table of Q (from 0 to 100, in increments of 10), P(QD), P(QS), and P(QS)+T.

b.   Graph of the demand curve, P(QD); supply curve before tariff, P(QS); and supply curve after tariff, P(QS)+T.

c.   What is equilibrium price and quantity before and after the tariff?

d.   What is the protective effect and revenue effect of the tariff?

43.   ECONOMIC IMPACT OF A TARIFF

Same as Exercise 42, except the tariff is set at $40 rather than $20.

44.   ECONOMIC IMPACT OF A TARIFF

Same as Exercise 42, except the tariff is set at $60 rather than $20.

45.   LEASE PAYMENT

Create a lease payment schedule based on the following data. Show the payment, interest expense, amortization of principal, and carrying value at December 31 for each year: Year 1 to Year 5.

Carrying value Jan. 1, Year 1	$20,000
Beginning of lease term	Jan. 1, 19Y1
Effective Interest	12%
Term of lease	5 years
Payment, beginning 12/31/Y1	$ 5,548

46.   FINANCIAL STATEMENTS

Examine Exhibits A and B. Exhibit A summarizes the eleven transactions of Gary Lyon, CPA, for the month of April 19X1. Suppose Lyon has completed the first seven transactions only and needs a bank loan on April 21, 19X1. The vice president of the bank requires financial statements to support all loan requests.

Prepare the income statement, statement of owner's equity, and balance sheet that Gary Lyon would present to the banker after completing the first seven transactions on April 21, 19X1. Exhibit B shows the financial statements on April 30. [DE1-10]

EXHIBIT A
Analysis of Transactions of Gary Lyon, CPA

Assets

	Cash	+	Receivable	+	Supplies	+	Land		
(1)	+ 50,000								
Bal.	50,000								
(2)	- 40,000						+40,000		
Bal.	10,000						40,000		
(3)					+500				
Bal.	10,000				500		40,000		
(4)	+ 5,500								
Bal.	15,000				500		40,000		
(5)			+3,000						
Bal.	15,000		3,000		500		40,000		
(6)	- 1,100								
	- 1,200								
	- 400								
Bal.	12,800		3,000		500		40,000		
(7)	- 400								
Bal.	12,400		3,000		500		40,000		
(8)	Not a transaction of the business								
(9)	+ 1,000		- 1,000						
Bal.	13,400		2,000		500		40,000		
(10)	+22,000						- 22,000		
Bal.	35,400		2,000		500		18,000		
(11)	- 2,100								
Bal.	33,300		2,000		500		18,000	=	53,800

EXHIBIT A (cont.)

	Liabilities	+	Owner's Equity	Type of Owner's Equity Transaction
	Accounts Payable	+	Gary Lyon, Capital	
(1)			+ 50,000	*Owner investment*
Bal.			50,000	
(2)				
Bal.			50,000	
(3)	+ 500			
Bal	500		50,000	
(4)			+ 5,500	*Service revenue*
Bal.	500		55,500	
(5)			+ 3,000	*Service revenue*
Bal.	500		58,500	
(6)			- 1,100	*Rent expense*
			- 1,200	*Salary expense*
			- 400	*Utilities expense*
Bal.	500		55,800	
(7)	- 400			
Bal.	100		55,800	
(8)				
(9)				
Bal.	100		55,800	
(10)				
Bal.	100		55,800	
(11)			- 2,100	*Owner withdrawal*
	100		53,700	= 53,800

EXHIBIT B
Financial Statements of Gary Lyon, CPA

Gary Lyon, CPA
Income Statement
Month Ended April 30, 19X1

Revenue		
Service revenue		$8,500
Expense		
Salary expense	$1,200	
Rent expense	1,100	
Utilities	400	
Total expenses		2,700
Net income		$5,800

Gary Lyon
Statement of Owner's Equity
Month Ended April 30, 19X1

Gary Lyon, capital, April 1, 19X1	$ 0
Add: Investments by owner	50,000
Net income for the month	5,800
. . . .	55,800
Less: Withdrawals by owner	(2,100)
Gary Lyon, capital, April 30, 19X1	$53,700

Gary Lyon, CPA
Balance Sheet
April 30, 19X1

Assets		Liabilities	
Cash	$33,300	Accounts payable	$ 100
Accounts receivable	2,000		
Office supplies	500	**Owner's Equity**	
Land	18,000	Gary Lyon, capital	53,700
		Total liabilities and	
Total assets	$53,800	owner's equity	$53,800

Gary Lyon, CPA
Statement of Cash Flows*
Month Ended April 30, 19X1

Cash flows from **operating** activities:		
Receipts:		
Collections from customers ($5,500 + $1,000).		$ 6,500
Payments:		
To suppliers ($1,100 + $400 + $400)..........	$(1,900)	
To employees.................................	(1,200)	(3,100)
Net cash inflow from operating activities.		3,400
Cash flows from **investing** activities:		
Acquisition of land.........................	$(40,000)	
Sale of land.................................	22,000	
Net cash outflow from financing		(18,000)
Cash flows from financing activities:		
Investment by owner	$ 50,000	
Withdrawal by owner	(2,100)	
Net cash inflow from financing activities.		47,900
Net increase in cash...........................		$33,300
Cash balance, April 1, 19X1....................		0
Cash balance, April 30, 19X1...................		$33,300

*Refer to your textbook for more information regarding this statement.

47.   INCOME STATEMENT

On-Point Delivery Service has just completed operations for the year ended December 31, 19X3. This is the third year of operations for the company. As the proprietor of the business, you want to know how well the business performed during the year. You also wonder where the business stands financially at the end of the year. To address these questions, you have assembled the following data:

Salary expense	$32,000	Insurance expense	$ 4,000
Accounts payable	7,000	Service revenue	91,000
Owner, capital		Accounts receivable	17,000
December 31, 19X2	13,000	Supplies expense	1,000
Supplies	2,000	Cash	5,000
Withdrawals by owner	36,000	Fuel expense	6,000
Rent expense	8,000		

Prepare the income statement of On-Point Delivery Service for the year ended December 31, 19X3. Follow the format shown in Exhibit B of Exercise 46. The income statement will measure the business's performance for the year. [DE1-15]

48.   STATEMENT OF OWNERS' EQUITY

Use the data in the exercise above to prepare the statement of owner's equity of On-Point Delivery Service for the year ended December 31, 19X3. Follow the format shown in Exhibit B of Exercise 46. Compute the net income from the data provided in the exercise above. [DE1-16].

49.   T-ACCOUNTS AND TRIAL BALANCE

Refer to the following transactions of Wellness Health Club.

Wellness Health Club Transactions

Wellness Health Club engaged in the following transactions during March 19X3, its first month of operations:

Mar. 1   Lou Stryker invested $45,000 of cash to start the business.
   2   Purchased office supplies of $200 on account.
   4   Paid $40,000 cash for a building to use as a future office.
   6   Performed service for customers and received cash, $2,000.
   9   Paid $100 on accounts payable.

Mar. 17   Performed service for customers on account, $1,600.
    23   Received $1,200 cash from a customer on account.
    31   Paid the following expenses: salary, $1,200; rent, $500.

Record the preceding transactions in the journal of Wellness Health Club. Key transactions by date and include an explanation for each entry. Use the following accounts: Cash; Accounts Receivable; Office Supplies; Building; Accounts Payable; Lou Stryker, Capital; Service Revenue; Salary Expense; Rent Expense. [Hint: For help, refer to the example file, GLEDGER].

1.   After journalizing the above transactions, post the entries to the ledger, using T-account format. Key transactions by date. Date the ending balance of each account Mar. 31.
2.   Prepare the trial balance of Wellness Health Club at March 31, 19X3. [E2-6]

50.   TRIAL BALANCE & INCOME STATEMENT

The following trial balance for Cincinnati Landscaping Service does not balance:

Cincinnati Landscaping Service
Trial Balance
June 30, 19X2

Cash.....................................	$ 2,000	
Accounts receivable..............	10,000	
Supplies................................	900	
Equipment............................	3,600	
Land.....................................	46,000	
Accounts payable...................		$ 4,000
Note payable..........................		22,000
Margo Schotte, capital...........		31,600
Margo Schotte, withdrawals..	2,000	
Service revenue......................		6,500
Salary expense.......................	2,100	
Rent expense.........................	1,000	
Advertising expense...............	500	
Utilities expense....................	400	
Total.....................................	$68,500	$64,100

The following errors were detected:
   a. The cash balance is understated by $700.
   b. The cost of the land was $43,000, not $46,000.
   c. A $200 purchase of supplies on account was neither journalized nor posted.
   d. A $2,800 credit to Service Revenue was not posted.
   e. Rent expense of $200 was erroneously posted as a credit rather than a debit.
   f. The balance of Advertising Expense is $600, but on the trial balance it was $500.
   g. A $300 debit to Accounts Receivable was posted as $30.
   h. The balance of Utilities Expense is overstated by $70.
   i. A $900 debit to the Withdrawals account was posted as a debit to Margo Schotte, Capital.

1. Prepare the correct trial balance at June 30. Journal entries are not required.
2. Prepare the company's income statement for the month ended June 30, 19X2, in order to determine Cincinnati Landscaping Service's net income or net loss for the month. Refer to Exhibit B of Exercise 46 if needed. [P2-5B]

51.   PREPARATION OF ADJUSTED TRIAL BALANCE

The adjusted trial balance of Total Express Service is incomplete. Enter the adjustment amounts directly in the adjustment columns. Service Revenue is the only account affected by more than one adjustment. [E3-9]

	Trial Balance		Adjustments		Adjusted Trial Balance	
TOTAL EXPRESS SERVICE Preparation of Adjusted Trial Balance May 31, 19X2						
	Dr.	Cr.	Dr.	Cr.	Dr.	Cr.
Cash	3,600				3,000	
Accounts receivable	6,500				7,100	
Supplies	1,040				800	
Office furniture	32,300				32,300	
Accumulated depreciation		14,040				14,400
Salary payable						900
Unearned revenue		900				690
Capital		26,360			6,000	26,360
Owner's withdrawals	6,000					
Service revenue		11,630			3,590	12,440
Salary expense	2,690				1,400	
Rent expense	1,400				360	
Depreciation expense					240	
Supplies expense						
	52,930	52,930			54,790	54,790

52. FINANCIAL STATEMENTS AND RELATED QUESTIONS

Below is the adjusted trial balance of Tradewind Travel Designers at December 31, 19x6.

Tradewind Travel Designers
Adjusted Trial Balance
December 31, 19X6

Cash	$ 1,320	
Accounts receivable	8,920	
Supplies	2,300	
Prepaid rent	1,600	
Office equipment	20,180	
Accumulated depreciation-office equipment		$ 4,350
Office furniture	37,710	
Accumulated depreciation-office furniture		4,870
Accounts payable		3,640
Property tax payable		1,100
Interest payable		830
Unearned service revenue		620
Note payable		13,500
Gary Gillen, capital		26,090
Gary Gillen, withdrawals	29,000	
Service revenue		124,910
Depreciation expense-office equipment	6,680	
Depreciation expense-office furniture	2,370	
Salary expense	39,900	
Rent expense	17,400	
Interest expense	3,100	
Utilities expense	2,670	
Insurance expense	3,180	
Supplies expense	2,950	
Total	$179,910	$179,910

Prepare Tradewind's 19X6 income statement and statement of owner's equity and year-end balance sheet. List expenses in decreasing order on the income statement and show total liabilities on the balance sheet.

1. Which financial statement reports Tradewind Travel's results of operations? Were operations successful during 19X6? Cite specifics from the financial statements to support your evaluation.

2.   Which statement reports the company's financial position? Does Tradewind's financial position look strong or weak? Give the reason for your evaluation. [P3-6A]

53.   POST-CLOSING TRIAL BALANCE

After closing its accounts at December 31, 19X6, Sprint Corporation had the following account balances (adapted) with amounts given in millions:

Property and equipment	$10,464	Long-term liabilities	$5,119
Cash	1,150	Other assets	2,136
Service revenue	-0-	Accounts receivable	2,464
Owners' equity	8,520	Total expenses	-0-
Other current assets	739	Accounts payable	1,027
Short-term notes payable	200	Other current liabilities . .	2,087

Prepare Sprint's post-closing trial balance at December 31, 19X6. List accounts in proper order, like the trial balance shown below. [DE4-15]

Gary Lyon, CPA
Postclosing Trial Balance
April 30, 19X1

Cash	$24,800	
Accounts receivable	2,500	
Supplies	400	
Prepaid rent	2,000	
Furniture..........................	16,500	
Accumulated depreciation		$ 275
Accounts payable		13,100
Salary payable		950
Unearned service revenue		300
Gary Lyon, capital		31,575
Total	$46,200	$46,200

54.   TRIAL BALANCE AND WORKSHEET

The trial balance of Goldsmith Testing Service follows:

Goldsmith Testing Service
Trial Balance
September 30, 19X6

Cash	$ 3,560	
Accounts receivable	3,440	
Prepaid rent	1,200	
Supplies	3,390	
Equipment	32,600	
Accumulated depreciation		$ 2,840
Accounts payable		3,600
Salary payable		
L. Goldsmith, capital		36,030
L. Goldsmith, withdrawals	3,000	
Service revenue		7,300
Depreciation expense		
Salary expense	1,800	
Rent expense		
Utilities expense	780	
Supplies expense		
Total	$49,770	$49,770

Additional information at September 30, 19X6:

Accrued service revenue, $210.
Depreciation, $40.
Accrued salary expense, $500.
Prepaid rent expired, $600.
Supplies used, $1,650.

Complete Goldsmith's worksheet (as shown on the following page) for September 19X6.
[E4-1]

Spreadsheet Exercises

Worksheet Started:

Goldsmith Testing Service
Work Sheet
Month Ended September 30, 19X6

Account Title	Trial Balance Dr.	Trial Balance Cr.	Adjustments Dr.	Adjustments Cr.	Adjusted Trial Balance Dr.	Adjusted Trial Balance Cr.	Income Statement Dr.	Income Statement Cr.	Balance Sheet Dr.	Balance Sheet Cr.
Cash										
Accounts receivable										
Prepaid rent										
Supplies										
Equipment										
Accumulated depreciation										
Accounts payable										
Salary payable										
L. Goldsmith, capital										
L. Goldsmith, withdrawals										
Service revenue										
Depreciation expense										
Salary expense										
Rent expense										
Utilities expense										
Supplies expense										
Totals										
Net income										
Totals (IS, BS)										

55. BALANCE SHEET

Use the data shown below to prepare Dell Computer's balance sheet at January 31, 19X5. Use the report format with all headings and list accounts in proper order. [DE5-16]

Dell Computer Corporation

Dell Computer Corporation reported these figures in its January 31, 19X5 financial statements (adapted, and in millions):

Cash	$ 43	Other assets (long-term)	$ 7
Total operating expenses . . .	589	Other current liabilities	304
Accounts payable	447	Property and equipment	208
Owners' equity	652	Net sales revenue	3,475
Long-term liabilities	191	Other current assets	596
Inventory	293	Accounts receivable	538
Cost of goods sold	2,737	Accumulated depreciation . . .	91

56. FINANCIAL RATIOS

Refer to the Dell Computer situation shown above. Compute Dell's gross margin percentage and rate of inventory turnover for 19X5. One year earlier, at January 31, 19X4, Dell's inventory balance was $220 million. [DE5-17]

57. CASH DISBURSEMENTS

During February, PanAm Imports had the following transactions:

Feb.	3	Paid $392 on account to Marquis Corp. net of an $8 discount for an earlier purchase of inventory.
	6	Purchased inventory for cash, $1,267.
	11	Paid $375 for supplies.
	15	Purchased inventory on credit from Monroe Corporation, $774.
	16	Paid $4,062 on account to LaGrange Associates; there was no discount.
	21	Purchased furniture for cash, $960.
	26	Paid $3,910 on account to Graff Software for an earlier purchase of inventory. The discount was $90.
	27	Made a semiannual interest payment of $800 on a long-term note payable. The entire payment was for interest.

1. Prepare a cash disbursement journal similar to the one illustrated below. As shown, the check number (Ck. No.) and posting reference (Post. Ref.) columns are not included.
2. Record the transactions in the journal. Which transaction should not be recorded in the cash disbursements journal? In what journal does it belong?
3. Total the amount columns of the journal. Determine that the total debits equal the total credits. [E6-10]

Solution Started:

Cash Disbursements Journal					
		Debits		Credits	
Date	Account Debited	Other Accounts	Accounts Payable	Inventory	Cash
Feb. 3	Marquis Corp.		400	8	92

58. BANK RECONCILIATION

D.J. Hunter's checkbook lists the following:

Date	Check No.	Item	Check	Deposit	Balance
9/1					$ 525
4	622	La Petite French Bakery	$ 19		506
9		Dividends Received		$ 116	622
13	623	General Tire Co.	43		579
14	624	Exxon Oil Co.	58		521
18	625	Cash	50		471
26	626	Fellowship Bible Church	25		446
28	627	Bent Tree Apartments	275		171
30		Paycheck		1,800	1,971

Hunter's September bank statement shows the following:

Balance			$525
Add: Deposits			116
Deduct checks:	No.	Amount	
	622	$19	
	623	43	
	624	68*	
	625	50	(180)
Other charges:			
Printed checks		$ 8	
Service charge		12	(20)
Balance			$441

*This is the correct amount for check number 624.

Prepare Hunter's bank reconciliation at September 30. [E7-6]

59.   CASH BUDGET

Suppose Sprint Incorporated, the long-distance telephone company, is preparing its cash budget for 19X4. The company ended 19X3 with $126 million, and top management forsees the need for a cash balance of at least $125 million to pay all bills as they come due in 19X4.

Collections from customers are expected to total $11,813 million during 19X4, and payments for the cost of services and products should reach $6,166 million. Operating expense payments are budgeted at $2,744 million.

During 19X4, Sprint expects to invest $1,826 million in new equipment, $275 million in the company's cellular division, and to sell older assets for $116 million. Debt payments scheduled for 19X4 will total $597 million. The company forecasts net income of $890 million for 19X4 and plans to pay $338 million to its owners.

Prepare Sprint's cash budget for 19X4. Will the budgeted level of cash receipts leave Sprint with the desired ending cash balance of $125 million, or will the company need additional financing? [E7-13]

60.   STATEMENT OF CASH FLOWS

The Home Depot, Inc. is the world's largest home improvement retailer. One of the company's great strengths is its cash flow from operations. The Home Depot has been able to grow rapidly without having to borrow heavily. This problem will sharpen your understanding of cash flows reporting.

At January 31, 19X7, end of the company's fiscal year, The Home Depot reported the following items (adapted) in its financial statements (amounts in millions):

Net sales	$19,536	Notes receivable	$39,518
Cash	146	Loaned out money on	
Cash receipts of interest		notes receivable	1,342
(same as interest revenue) .	26	Merchandise inventories ...	2,708
Buildings	2,470	Accounts receivable, net ...	388
Cost of goods sold	14,101	Collections on notes receivable	16,539
Collections from customers .	19,473	All other expenses	4,523

1.   Show how The Home Depot could have reported the relevant items from this list on its statement of cash flows for the year ended January 31, 19X7. Include a heading for the statement.
2.   Compute The Home Depot's net income for the year. Was all the net income received in cash? How can you tell? [P8-9B]

61.   INCOME STATEMENT

Supply the missing income statement amounts, a-g, for each of the following companies:

Company	Net Sales	Beginning Inventory	Net Purchases	Ending Inventory	Cost of Goods Sold	Gross Margin
A	$92,800	$12,500	$62,700	$19,400	(a)	$37,000
B	(b)	27,450	93,000	(c)	$94,100	51,200
C	94,700	(d)	54,900	22,600	59,400	(e)
D	98,600	10,700	(f)	8,200	(g)	47,100

Prepare the income statement for Company D, which uses the periodic inventory system. Company D's operating expenses for the year were $32,100. [E9-6]

62. PERPETUAL INVENTORY RECORD

Piazza Music World carries a large inventory of guitars, keyboards, and other musical instruments. Because each item is expensive, Piazza uses a perpetual inventory system. Company records indicate the following for a particular line of Casio keyboards:

Date	Item	Quantity	Unit Cost
May 1	Balance	5	$90
6	Sale	3	
8	Purchase	11	95
17	Sale	4	
30	Sale	1	

Determine the amounts that Piazza should report for ending inventory and cost of goods sold by the FIFO method. Prepare the perpetual inventory record for Casio keyboards, using the model below. [E9-8]

Perpetual Inventory Record – FIFO Cost

Hunting Galleries										
Item: Early American Chairs										
	Received			Sold			Balance			
Date	Qty.	Unit Cost	Total	Qty.	Unit Cost	Total	Qty.	Unit Cost	Total	
Nov. 1							10	$300	$3,000	
5				6	$300	$ 1,800	4	300	1,200	
7	25	$310	$7,750				4	300	1,200	
							25	310	7,750	
12				4	300	1,200				
				9	310	2,790	16	310	4,960	
26	25	320	8,000				16	310	4,960	
							25	320	8,000	
30				16	310	4,960				
				5	320	1,600	20	320	6,400	
Totals:	50		$15,750	40		$12,350	20		$6,400	

63.   INCOME STATEMENT, BALANCE SHEET, AND STATEMENT OF CASH FLOWS

Campbell Soup Company uses a perpetual inventory system and the LIFO method to determine the cost of its inventory. During a recent year, Campbell Soup reported the following items (adapted) in its financial statements (listed in alphabetical order, and with amounts given in millions of dollars)

Collections from customers	$7,255		Payments for inventory	$4,150
Cost of goods sold	4,264		Revenues, total	7,288
Other expenses	2,326		Total assets	6,315
Owners' equity	2,468		Total liabilities	3,847

1.   Prepare as much of Campbell Soup Company's statement of cash flows for the year ended July 31, 19X5, as you can. Include a complete heading.
2.   Prepare Campbell Soup Company's summary income statement for the year ended July 31, 19X5, complete with a heading.
3.   Prepare Campbell Soup Company's summary balance sheet at July 31, 19X5, complete with a heading. [E9-19]

64.   ALLOCATION OF COSTS IN LUMP-SUM PURCHASE

Advantage Leasing Company bought three used machines in a $40,000 lump-sum purchase. An independent appraiser valued the machines as follows:

Machine No.	Appraised Value
1	14,000
2	18,000
3	16,000

Advantage paid half in cash and signed a note payable for the remainder. Record the purchase in the journal, identifying each machine's individual cost in a separate Machine account. Round decimals to three places. [E10-3]

65.   PARTIAL BALANCE SHEET

Assume that Wilson Sporting Goods completed these selected transactions during December 19X6:

a.   Champs, a chain of sporting goods stores, ordered $15,000 of tennis and golf equipment. With its order, Champs sent a check for $15,000 in advance. Wilson will ship the goods on January 3, 19X7.

b. The December payroll of $195,000 is subject to employee withheld income tax of 9%, FICA tax of 8% (employee and employer), state unemployment tax of 5.4%, and federal unemployment tax of 0.8 percent. On December 31, Wilson pays employees but accrues all tax amounts.

c. Sales of $1,000,000 are subject to estimated warranty cost of 1.4 percent.

d. On December 2, Wilson signed a $100,000 note payable that requires annual payments of $20,000 plus 9% interest on the unpaid balance each December 2.

Classify each liability as current or long-term, and prepare a partial balance sheet showing liabilities above, as of December 31, 19X6. [E11-12]

66. SUMMARY OF LIQUIDATION TRANSACTIONS

Prior to liquidation, the accounting records of Pratt, Qualls, and Ramirez included the following balances and profit-and-loss sharing percentages:

	Cash	+	Noncash Assets	=	Liabilities	+	Capital Pratt (40%)	+	Qualls (30%)	Ramirez + (30%)
Balances before sale of assets	$8,000		$57,000		$19,000		$20,000		$15,000	$11,000

The partnership sold the noncash assets for $73,000, paid the liabilities, and disbursed the remaining cash to the partners. Complete the summary of transactions in the liquidation of the partnership. Use the same approach as illustrated below. [E12-10]

**Partnership Liquidation –
Sale of Assets at a Gain**

	Cash	+	Noncash Assets	=	Liabilities	+	Aviron (60%)	+	Bloch (20%)	+	Crane (20%)
Balance before sale of Assets	$ 10,000		$90,000		$30,000		$40,000		$20,000		$10,000
Sale of assets and sharing of gain	150,000		(90,000)				36,000		12,000		
Balances	160,000		-0-		30,000		76,000		32,000		22,000
Payment of liabilities .	(30,000)				(30,000)						
Balances	130,000		-0-		-0-		76,000		32,000		22,000
Disbursement of cash to partners	(130,000)						(76,000)		(32,000)		(22,000)
Balances	$ -0-	$	-0-	$	-0-	$	-0-	$	-0-	$	-0-

67.   FINANCIAL RATIO S

DuBois Furniture, Inc., reported these figures for 19X7 and 19X6:

	19X7	19X6
Income statement:		
Interest expense	$ 17,400,000	$7,100,000
Net income	12,000,000	18,700,000
Balance sheet:		
Total assets	351,000,000	317,000,000
Preferred stock, $1.30, no-par,		
100,000 shares issued and outstanding	2,500,000	2,500,000
Common stockholders' equity	164,000,000	151,000,000
Total stockholders' equity	166,500,000	153,500,000

Compute rate of return on total assets and rate of return on common stockholders' equity for 19X7. Do these rates of return suggest strength or weakness? Give your reason.
[E13-13]

68.   BALANCE SHEET, FINANCIAL RATIOS, AND RELATED QUESTIONS

The following accounts and related balances of Borzhov, Inc., are arranged in no particular order.

Accounts receivable, net ...$46,000		Interest expense	$ 6,100
Paid-in capital in excess		Property, plant, and	
Of par-common 19,000		equipment, net	261,000
Accrued liabilities 26,000		Common stock, $1 par,	
Long-term note payable 42,000		500,000 shares authorized,	
Inventory 81,000		236,000 shares issued ...	236,000
Dividends payable 9,000		Prepaid expenses	10,000
Retained earnings .... ?		Revenue from donation ...	6,000
Accounts payable 31,000		Common stockholders' equity,	
Trademark, net 9,000		June 30 , 19X1	222,000
Preferred stock, $0.10, no-par		Net income	31,000
10,000 shares authorized		Total assets, June 30, 19X1	404,000
and issued 27,000		Cash	13,000

1.   Prepare the company's classified balance sheet in the account format at June 30, 19X2. Use the accounting equation to compute Retained Earnings.

2. Compute rate of return on total assets and rate of return on common stockholders' equity for the year ended June 30, 19X2.

3. Do these rates of return suggest strength or weakness? Give your reason. [P13-6A]

69.   MULTIPLE-STEP INCOME STATEMENT

Graz Corporation's accounting records contain the following information for 19X8 operations:

Sales revenue.............................	$380,000
Operating expenses (including income tax)..............	93,000
Cumulative effect of change in depreciation method (debit)......	(7,000)
Cost of good sold........................	245,000
Loss on discounted operations....	50,000
Income tax expense- extraordinary gain......................	6,000
Income tax saving-change in depreciation method..............	3,000
Income tax saving-loss on discontinued operations........	20,000
Extraordinary gain......................	15,000

Prepare a multiple-step income statement for 19X8. Omit earnings per share. Was 19X8 a good year, a fair year, or a bad year for Graz Corporation? Explain your answer in terms of the outlook for 19X9. [E14-8]

70.   BOND AMORTIZATION SCHEDULE

Atlas Airlines, Inc., issued $600,000 of a 8 3/8% (0.08375), five-year bonds payable when the market interest rate was 9 1/2% (0.095). Atlas pays interest annually at year end. The issue price of the bonds was $574,082.

Create a spreadsheet model to prepare a schedule to amortize the discount on these bonds. Use the effective-interest method of amortization. Round to the nearest dollar, and format your answer as follows. [E15-7]

1	A	B	C	D	E	F
2						Bond
3		Interest	Interest	Discount	Discount	Carrying
4	Date	Payment	Expense	Amortization	Balance	Amount
5	1-1-X1				$____	$574,082
6	12-31-X1	$____	$____	$____			$____
7	12-31-X2									
8	12-31-X3									
9	12-31-X4									
10	12-31-X5									
		600000*.08375	+F5*.095	+C6-B6	600000-F5	+F5+D6

71.   STATEMENT OF CASH FLOWS -- INVESTING ACTIVITIES

During fiscal year 19X5, The Home Depot which operates over 400 home improvement centers throughout the United States, reported net income of $604 million and paid $162 million to acquire other businesses. Home Depot paid $1,103 million to open new stores and sold property, plant, and equipment for $50 million. The company purchased long-term investments in stocks and bonds at a cost of $94 million and sold other long-term investments for $454 million. During the year, the company also cashed in other investments for $96 million.

Prepare the investing activities section of The Home Depot's statement of cash flows. Based on The Home Depot's investing activities, does it appear that the company is growing or shrinking? How can you tell? [E16-10]

72. STATEMENT OF CASH FLOWS

The income statement and additional data of Boyce Computing Company follow:

Boyce Computing Company
Income Statement
Year Ended September 30, 19X2

Revenues:		
Sales revenue...............................		$237,000
Expenses:		
Cost of goods sold............................	103,000	
Salary expense....................................	45,000	
Depreciation expense.........................	29,000	
Rent expense.....................................	11,000	
Interest expense.................................	2,000	
Income tax expense............................	9,000	199,000
Net income.......................................		$ 38,000

Additional data during fiscal year 19X2:

a.   Collections from customers were $7,000 more than sales.

b.   Payments to suppliers were $5,000 less than the sum of cost of goods sold plus rent expense.

c.   Payment to employees were $1,000 more than salary expense.

d.   Interest expense and income tax expense equal their cash amounts.

e.   Acquisition of equipment is $116,000. Of this amount, $101,000 was paid in cash, $15,000 by signing a long-term note payable. Boyce sold no equipment during fiscal year 19X2.

f.   Proceeds from sales of land, $14,000.

g.   Proceeds from issuance of common stock, $35,000.

h.   Payment of long-term note payable, $20,000.

i.   Payment of dividends, $10,000.

j.   Decrease in cash balance, $4,000.

1.   Prepare Boyce Computing Company's statement of cash flows and accompanying schedule of noncash investing and financing activities. Report operating activities by the **direct** method.

2.   Evaluate Boyce Computing Company's cash flows for the year. In your evaluation, mention all three categories of cash flows, and give the reason for your evaluation. [E17-6]

73.   HORIZONTAL ANALYSIS OF INCOME STATEMENTS

Prepare a horizontal analysis of the following comparative income statement of Dynasty International. Round percentage changes to the nearest one-tenth percent (three decimal places):

Dynasty International
Comparative Income Statement
Years Ended December 31, 19X9 and 19X8

	19X9	19X8
Total revenue...............................	$410,000	$373,000
Expenses:		
Cost of goods sold...................	$202,000	$188,000
Selling and general expenses..	98,000	93,000
Interest expense.......................	7,000	4,000
Income tax expense................	42,000	37,000
Total expenses........................	349,000	322,000
Net income...............................	$ 61,000	$ 51,000

Why did net income increase by a higher percentage than total revenues during 19X9?
[E18-2]

74.   COST OF GOODS MANUFACTURED AND COST OF GOODS SOLD

Compute cost of goods manufactured and cost of goods sold from the following amounts.
[E19-6]

	Beginning of Year	End of Year
Materials inventory	$22,000	$28,000
Work-in-process inventory	38,000	30,000
Finished-goods inventory	18,000	25,000
Purchases of raw materials		78,000
Direct labor		82,000
Indirect labor		15,000
Insurance on plant		9,000
Depreciation-plant building and equipment		16,000
Repairs and maintenance-plant		4,000
Marketing expenses		77,000
General and administrative expenses		29,000
Income tax expense		30,000

75.   INCOME STATEMENT

Prepare an income statement for the company in the exercise above. Assume that it sold 27,000 units of its product at a price of $14 during the current year. [E19-7]

76.   WORK-IN-PROCESS AND RELATED QUESTIONS

August production generated the following activity in the Work-in-Process Inventory account of Zumikazi Manufacturing Company:

	Work in Process Inventory	
August 1 Balance	10,000	
Direct materials used	28,000	
Direct labor charged to jobs	31,000	
Manufacturing overhead allocated to jobs	11,000	

Completed production, not yet recorded, consists of Jobs B-78, G-65, and Y- 11, with total costs of $16,000, $27,000, and $33,000, respectively.

1.   Compute the cost of work in process at August 31.
2.   Prepare the journal entry for production completed in August.
3.   Prepare the journal entry to record the sale (on credit) of Job G-65 for $41,000. Also make the cost-of-goods-sold entry.
4.   What is the gross margin on Job G-65? What other costs does this gross margin have to cover? [E20-5]

77. COMPUTE EQUIVALENT UNITS -- FIFO

Selected production and cost data of Harmon's Hardwood Flooring, follows for May 19X9:

| | Flow of Physical Units | |
| | Sanding | Finishing |
Flow of Production	Department	Department
Units to account for:		
Beginning work in process, April 30	20,000	6,000
Transferred in during May	70,000	80,000
Total physical units to account for	90,000	86,000
Units accounted for:		
Completed and transferred out during May:		
From beginning inventory	20,000	6,000
Started and completed during May	60,000	75,000
Work-in-process, May 31	10,000	5,000
Total physical units accounted for	90,000	86,000

Harmon's uses FIFO process costing.

1. Fill in the blanks:

    a. On April 30, the Sanding Department beginning work-in-process inventory was 80% complete as to materials and 90% complete as to conversion costs. This means that for the beginning inventory, ___% of the materials and ___ % of the conversion costs were added during May.

    b. On May 31, the Sanding Department ending work-in-process inventory was 60% complete as to materials and 40% complete as to conversion costs. This means that for the ending, inventory ___ % of the materials and ___ % of the conversion costs were added during May.

    c. On April 30, the Finishing Department beginning work-in-process inventory was 33 1/3% complete as to materials and 60% complete as to conversion costs. This means that for the beginning inventory ___ % of the materials and ___ % of the conversion costs were added during May.

    d. On May 31, the Finishing Department ending work-in-process inventory, was 70% complete as to materials and 60% complete as to Conversion costs. This means that for the ending inventory ___ % of the materials and ___ % of the conversion costs were added during May.

2. Use the Flow of Production data and the information in requirement 1 to compute

the equivalent units for transferred-in costs (if necessary), direct materials, and conversion costs for both the Sanding Department and the Finishing Department. [E21-10]

78.   COMPUTE EQUIVALENT UNITS -- WEIGHTED AVERAGE

Repeat Requirement 2 of the exercise above for the Finishing Department, using the weighted-average method. [E21-11]

79.   GRAPH COST BEHAVIOR PATTERNS

Graph each of the following cost behavior patterns over a relevant range from 0 to 10,000 units:

a.   Variable expenses of $8 per unit

b.   Mixed expenses made up of fixed costs of $10,000 and variable costs of $3 per unit

c.   Fixed expenses of $35,000 [E22-1]

80.   CONTRIBUTION MARGIN INCOME STATEMENT

Saville Row Shirtmakers' April income statement follows:

Saville Row Shirtmakers
Income Statement
April 19XX

Sales revenue		$640,000
Cost of goods sold		448,000
Gross margin		192,000
Operating expenses:		
Marketing expense	$72,000	
General and administrative expense	42,000	114,000
Operating income		$ 78,000

Saville Row's cost of goods sold is a variable expense. Marketing expense is 20% fixed and 80% variable. General and administrative expense is 60% fixed and 40% variable. Prepare Saville Row's contribution margin income statement for April. Compute the expected increase in operating income to the nearest $1,000 if sales increase by $50,000. [E22-2]

81.   DEPARTMENTAL INCOME STATEMENT

Portland Gear has two departments, Electronics and Industrial. The company's income statement for 19X9 appears as follows:

Net sales.............................	$350,000
Cost of goods sold..............	116,000
Gross margin	234,000
Operating expenses:...........	
Salaries expense	$ 75,000
Depreciation expense	15,000
Advertising expense	6,000
Other expenses	10,000
Total operating expenses..	106,000
Operating income...............	$128,000

Sales are Electronics, $136,000 and Industrial, $214,000. Cost of goods sold is distributed $42,000 to Electronics and $74,000 to Industrial. Salaries are traced directly to departments: Electronics, $33,000; Industrial, $42,000. Electronics accounts for 80% of advertising. Depreciation is allocated on the basis of square footage: Electronics has 20,000 square feet; Industrial has 40,000 square feet. Other expenses are allocated based on the number of employees. An equal number of employees work in each of the two departments.

1.   Prepare departmental income statements that show revenues, expenses, and operating income for each of the company's two departments.
2.   In a departmental performance report, which are the most important expenses for evaluating Portland Gear's department managers? Give your reason. [E23-10]

82.   FLEXIBLE BUDGET

Kandlestix Company, sells its main product, an elaborate candle, for $7.50 each. Its variable cost is $2 per candle. Fixed expenses are $200,000 per month for volumes up to 60,000 candles. Above 60,000 candles, monthly fixed expenses are $240,000.
       Prepare a monthly flexible budget for the product, showing sales, variable expenses, fixed expenses, and operating income or loss for volume levels of 40,000, 50,000, and 70,000 candles. [E24-1]

83.   GRAPH TOTAL LOST LINE

Graph the flexible budget total cost line for Kandlestix Company in the exercise above.   .
Show total costs for volume levels of 40,000, 50,000, and 70,000 candles. [E24-2]

84.   COST ALLOCATION RATES

Chromium Ltd. uses activity-based costing for its manufacturing process. Company
managers have identified four manufacturing activities: materials handling, machine
setup, insertion of parts, and finishing. The budgeted activity costs for 19X8 and their
allocation bases are as follows:

Activity	Total Budgeted Cost	Allocation Base
Materials handling	$12,000	Number of parts
Machine setup	2,400	Number of setups
Insertion of parts	24,000	Number of parts
Finishing	60,000	Finishing direct labor-hours
Total	$98,400	

Chromium expects to produce 2,000 chrome wheels during the year. The wheels are
expected to use 12,000 parts, require 6 setups, and consume 1,000 hours of finishing
time.

1.   Compute the cost allocation rate for each activity.
2.   Compute the indirect manufacturing cost of each wheel. [E25-1]

85.   BUDGETED COSTS, ABC COST PER UNIT

Several years after reengineering its production process, Chromex hired a new controller,
Rebecca Steinberg. She developed an ABC system very similar to the one used by
Chromex's chief rival, Chromium, Ltd., described above. Part of the reason Steinberg
developed the ABC system was that Chromex's profits had been declining, even though
the company had shifted its product mix toward the product that had appeared most
profitable under the old system. Before adopting the new ABC system, Chromex had
used a direct labor hour single-allocation-base system that was developed 20 years ago.

For 19X8, Chromex's budgeted ABC allocation rates are:

Activity	Allocation Base	Cost Allocation Rate
Materials handling	Number of parts	$ 1.25 per part
Machine setup	Number of setups	300.00 per setup
Insertion of parts	Number of parts	3.00 per part
Finishing	Finishing direct labor-hours	70.00 per hour

The number of parts is now a feasible allocation base because Chromex recently purchased bar coding technology. Chromex produces two wheel models: standard and deluxe. Budgeted data for 19X8 are as follows:

	Standard	Deluxe
Parts per Unit	50.0	70.0
Setups Per 1,000 units	3.0	3.0
Finishing direct labor hours per unit	0.2	1.0
Total direct labor hours per unit	2.0	3.0

The company's managers expect to produce 1,000 units of each model during the year.

1. Compute the total budgeted cost for 19X8.
2. Compute the ABC cost per unit of each model.
3. Using Chromex's old direct labor hour single allocation-base system, compute the (single) allocation rate based on direct labor hours. Use this rate to determine the cost per wheel for each model under the old single-allocation-base method. [E25-2]

86.   MANUFACTURING COST BASED ON ABC UNIT COST

Refer to the exercise above. For 19X9, Chromex's managers have decided to use the same conversion costs per wheel that they computed in 19X8. In addition to the unit conversion costs, the following data are budgeted for the company's standard and deluxe models for 19X9:

	Standard	Deluxe
Sale price	$110.00	$155.00
Direct materials	15.00	25.00

Because of limited machine hour capacity, Chromex can produce either 2,000 standard wheels or 2,000 deluxe wheels.

1.   If the managers rely on the ABC unit cost data computed in the exercise above, which model will they produce? Show support for your answer. (All non-manufacturing costs are the same for both models.)

2.   If the managers rely on the single-allocation-base cost data, which model will they produce? Show support for your answer.

3.   Which course of action will yield more income for Chromex? Show support for your answer. [E25-3]

87.   PRODUCT MIX ANALYSIS

Four Seasons Fashions sells both designer and moderately priced women's wear. Profits have fluctuated recently, and top management is deciding which product line to emphasize. Accountants have provided the following data:

	Per Item	
	Designer	Moderately Priced
Average sale price	$200	$80
Average variable expenses	70	24
Average contribution margin	$130	$56
Average fixed expenses (allocated)	20	10
Average gross margin	$110	$46

The Four Seasons store in Boca Raton, Florida, has 10,000 square feet of floor space. If it emphasizes moderately priced goods, 500 items can be displayed in the store. In contrast, if it emphasizes designer wear, only 200 designer items can be displayed for sale. These numbers are also the average monthly sales in units.

Prepare an analysis to show which product to emphasize. [E26-4]

88.   MAKE OR BUY ANALYSIS

Skiptronics Industrial Controls manufactures an electronic control that it uses in its final product. The electronic control has the following manufacturing costs per unit:

Direct materials	$ 5.00
Direct labor	1.00
Variable overhead	1.50
Fixed overhead	4.00
Manufacturing product cost	$11.50

Another company has offered to sell Skiptronics the electronic control for $8 per unit. If Skiptronics buys the control from the outside supplier, the manufacturing facilities that will be idled cannot be used for any other purpose. Should Skiptronics make or buy the electronic controls? Explain the difference between correct analysis and incorrect analysis of this decision. [E26-5]

89.   BEST USE OF FACILITIES ANALYSIS

Refer to the exercise above. Skiptronics needs 90,000 electronic controls. By purchasing them from the outside supplier, Skiptronics can use its idle facilities to manufacture another product that will contribute $75,000 to operating income. Identify the *incremental* costs that Skiptronics will incur to acquire 90,000 electronic controls under three alternative plans. Which plan makes the best use of Skiptronic's facilities? Support your answer. [E26-6]

SOLUTIONS
to
Odd-Numbered Exercises 1-45

1. INCOME STATEMENT

FILE IDENTIFICATION AREA:

Name:	Tracy Smith
Date Created:	June 20, 2000
Filename:	E1.XLS

INPUT AREA:

Sales	$200,000

OUTPUT AREA:

CHRIS RAY'S CARD SHOP
INCOME STATEMENT
FYE 12/31/99

Sales	$200,000
Cost of Sales	$80,000

Gross profit	$120,000
Operating Expenses	$30,000

Net income	$90,000

= = = = = = = = = = =

3.   DOUBLE-ENTRY ACCOUNTING

IDENTIFICATION AREA:

Filename: E3.xls   P. 1 OF 4
Designer:
Date:
Directions: Enter journal entries into the general ledger accounts.
             A trial balance and income statement are automatically
             prepared from the general ledger balances.

INPUT/OUTPUT AREA:

GENERAL LEDGER ACCOUNTS:

	No. 101	CASH	
Date |	Dr. |	Cr. |	Balance
Jan. 1	8,000		8,000
Jan. 1		1,500	6,500
Jan. 15	1,600		8,100
Jan. 25		375	7,725
Jan. 26		225	7,500
Jan. 31		4,000	3,500
			3,500
Ending Balance			3,500

	No. 102	ACCOUNTS RECEIVABLE	
Date ,	Dr. ,	Cr. ,	Balance
Jan. 10	3,200		3,200
Jan. 12	1,200		4,400
Jan. 15		1,600	2,800
Jan. 20	2,000		4,800
			4,800
Ending Balance			4,800

	No. 103	PREPAID RENT	
Date ,	Dr. ,	Cr. ,	Balance
Jan. 1	1,500		1,500
Jan. 31		500	1,000
			1,000
Ending Balance			1,000

3. continued

E3.xls   **Solution P. 2 of 4**

Date	Dr.	Cr.	Balance
	No. 104	OFFICE SUPPLIES	
Jan. 3	800		800
Jan. 31		400	400
			400
Ending Balance			400

Date	Dr.	Cr.	Balance
	No. 105	QUIPMENT	
Jan. 2	4,000		4,000
			4,000
			4,000
Ending Balance			4,000

Date	Dr.	Cr.	Balance
	No. 106	ACCUM. DEPRECIATION, OFFICE EQUIPMENT	
Jan. 31		150	150
			150
			150
Ending Balance			150

Date	Dr.	Cr.	Balance
	No. 201	ACCOUNTS PAYABLE	
Jan. 3		800	800
			800
			800
Ending Balance			800

Date	Dr.	Cr.	Balance
	No. 202	NOTES PAYABLE	
Jan. 2		4,000	4,000
			4,000
			4,000
Ending Balance			4,000

3. continued

E3.xls   **Solution P. 3 of 4**

No. 301	MARY SMITH, CAPITAL		
Date	Dr.	Cr.	Balance
Jan. 1		8,000	8,000
			8,000
Ending Balance			8,000

No. 302	MARY SMITH, WITHDRAWALS		
Date	Dr.	Cr.	Balance
Jan. 31	4,000		4,000
			4,000
Ending Balance			4,000

No. 401	CONSULTING FEES EARNED		
Date	Dr.	Cr.	Balance
Jan. 10		3,200	3,200
Jan. 12		1,200	4,400
Jan. 20		2,000	6,400
			6,400
Ending Balance			6,400

No. 501	DEP. EXPENSE, OFFICE EQUIPMENT		
Date	Dr.	Cr.	Balance
Jan. 31	150		150
			150
Ending Balance			150

3. continued

E3.xls   **Solution P. 4 of 4**

	No. 502	OFFICE SUPPLIES EXP.	
Date	Dr.	Cr.	Balance
Jan. 31	400		400
			400
Ending Balance			400

	No. 503	RENT EXPENSE	
Date	Dr.	Cr.	Balance
Jan. 31	500		500
			500
			500
Ending Balance			500

	No. 504	UTILITIES EXPENSE	
Date	Dr.	Cr.	Balance
Jan. 26	225		225
			225
			225
Ending Balance			225

	No. 505	TELEPHONE EXPENSE	
Date	Dr.	Cr.	Balance
Jan. 25	375		375
			375
			375
Ending Balance			375

5.   COST OF MERCHANDISE

FILE IDENTIFICATION AREA:

Name:
Date Created:
Filename: E5.xls

INPUT AREA:

List Price $5,000
Trade Discount   30%
Credit Terms   2 /   10   NET   30

OUTPUT AREA:

Amount Due If Paid After   10 days: $3,500
Amount Due If Paid Within   10 days: 3,430

Discount $70
                                          = = = = =

7.   TRACKING INVENTORY QUANTITY

FILE IDENTIFICATION AREA:

Name:
Date Created:
Filename: E7.xls

INPUT AREA:

Item #	Description	Quantity on hand	Quantity desired
--------------	------------------	----------------	----------------
100	HAMMER	8	30
200	SCREWDRIVER	26	20
300	SAW	57	45
400	WRENCH	34	20
500	PLIERS	5	15

OUTPUT AREA:

Item No	Description	Quantity on hand	Quantity desired	over or (under)
--------------	------------------ --	----------------	----------------	----------------
100	HAMMER	8	30	(22)
200	SCREWDRIVER	26	20	6
300	SAW	57	45	12
400	WRENCH	34	20	14
500	PLIERS	5	15	(10)

9.   STRAIGHT LINE DEPRECIATION

FILE IDENTIFICATION AREA:

Name:
Date Created:
Filename: E9.xls

INPUT AREA:

Cost of Asset   = $20,000
Salvage Value   = $2,000
Useful Life (Years)   =   10
Months Held This Year (1-12)   =   6

OUTPUT AREA:

DEPRECIATION EXPENSE   = $900
                                     = = =

11.   SUM-OF-THE-YEARS-DIGITS DEPRECIATION

FILE IDENTIFICATION AREA:

Name:
Date Created:
Filename: E11.xls

INPUT AREA:

COST:	$250,000
SALVAGE:	$24,000
LIFE:	10 YEARS
PERIOD:	4 YEARS

OUTPUT AREA:

DEPRECIATION EXPENSE FOR THIS YEAR: $28,764

              = = = = =

13.   BAD DEBT EXPENSE

FILE IDENTIFICATION AREA:

Name:
Date Created:
Filename: E13.xls

INPUT AREA:

Age of Accounts	A/R Balance	Percent Uncollectible
Under 30 days	$45,000	1%
30-60 days	$25,000	3%
61-120 days	$15,000	10%
Over 120 days	$10,000	30%

OUTPUT AREA:

Bad Debts Expense 1999: $5,700
                                     =======

15.   CASH BUDGET

FILE IDENTIFICATION AREA:

Name:
Date Created:
Filename: E15.xls

INPUT AREA:

	March	April
Cash Balance, Beginning	$10,000	
Cash Collections	$25,000	$15,000
Sale of Asset	$12,000	$0
Purchases	$12,000	$8,000
Operating Expenses	$5,500	$2,225

OUTPUT AREA:

	March	April
Cash Balance, Beginning	$10,000	$29,500
Cash Collections	$25,000	$15,000
Sale of Asset	$12,000	$0
Total Available	$47,000	$44,500
Cash Disbursements:		
Purchases	$12,000	$8,000
Operating Expenses	$5,500	$2,225
Total Disbursements	$17,500	$10,225
Cash Balance, Ending	$29,500	$34,275

17.   INTEREST EARNED

FILE IDENTIFICATION AREA:

Name:
Date Created:
Filename: E17.xls

INPUT AREA:

Principal   = $1,000
Interest Rate   =   7.0%
Time Held (Days)   =   61

OUTPUT AREA:

PRINCIPAL   *   INT. RATE   *   TIME HELD/360   INT. EARNED

     $1,000   *   7.00%   *   61 /360 $12

19.   WEIGHTED AVERAGE NUMBER OF SHARES OF STOCK

FILE IDENTIFICATION AREA:

Name:
Date Created:
Filename: E19.xls

INPUT AREA:

JAN - MAR	500
APR - JUL	1200
AUG	1000
SEPT - OCT	1800
NOV	1500
DEC	2000

OUTPUT AREA:

	# of shares	# of months	# of shares * # of months
JAN - MAR	500	3	1,500
APR - JUL	1200	4	4,800
AUG	1000	1	1,000
SEPT - OCT	1800	2	3,600
NOV	1500	1	1,500
DEC	2000	1	2,000
		12	14,400

WEIGHTED AVG. NO. OF SHARES O/S FOR YEAR: 1,200
                                                   ======

21.   JOINT COST ALLOCATION

FILE IDENTIFICATION AREA:

Name:
Date Created:
Filename: E21.xls

INPUT AREA:

Total costs: $600,000

PRODUCT	SALES VALUE AT SPLIT-OFF
A	$800,000
B	$500,000
C	$700,000

OUTPUT AREA:

	A	B	C	TOTAL
Sales value at split-off	$800,000	$500,000	$700,000	$2,000,000
Weights	40.00%	25%	35%	100%
Joint costs allocated	$240,000	$150,000	$210,000	$600,000

23.   AGING SALES INVOICES

FILE IDENTIFICATION AREA:

Name:
Date Created:
Filename: E23.xls

INPUT AREA:

Current Date: 11/15/99

UNCOLLECTED INVOICE #	DATE	AMOUNT	FIRM	TERM			
225	05/25/99	$950	BLUE	1	10 N	60
301	06/17/99	235	RED	2	10 N	60
302	07/02/99	340	RED	2	10 N	60
303	07/03/99	560	BLUE	1	10 N	60
307	08/18/99	270	PINK		N	60
309	09/15/99	880	PINK		N	30
312	09/22/99	1690	BLUE	1	10 N	60
317	10/02/99	120	PINK		N	30
318	10/03/99	490	PINK		N	30
319	10/07/99	460	BLUE	1	10 N	60

OUTPUT AREA:

Current Date: 11/15/99

UNCOLLECTED INVOICE #	DATE	AMOUNT	FIRM	TERM			DAYS O/S	DAYS PAST-DUE
225	05/25/99	$950	BLUE	1	10 N	60	174	114
301	06/17/99	235	RED	2	10 N	60	151	91
302	07/02/99	340	RED	2	10 N	60	136	76
303	07/03/99	560	BLUE	1	10 N	60	135	75
309	09/15/99	880	PINK		N	30	61	31
307	08/18/99	270	PINK		N	60	89	29
317	10/02/99	120	PINK		N	30	44	14
318	10/03/99	490	PINK		N	30	43	13
312	09/22/99	1690	BLUE	1	10 N	60	54	-6
319	10/07/99	460	BLUE	1	10 N	60	39	-21

Average Days						51	92.6	41.6

Note: A negative number means that the invoice is not past due.

25.   SALES BY PRODUCT TYPE

FILE IDENTIFICATION AREA:

Name:
Date Created:
Filename: E25.xls

INPUT AREA:

SALES SUMMARY REPORT BY PRODUCT TYPE
February

Product Type	Current Month Sales	Prior Month Sales	% Chg.	Year to Date Sales	Last Yr. Year to Date Sales	% Chg.
----	----	----	----	----	----	----
A	16	25	-36%	80	100	-20%
B	52	45	16%	260	234	11%
C	44	32	38%	220	154	43%
D	72	67	7%	360	333	8%
E	35	37	-5%	175	180	-3%

OUTPUT AREA:

SALES SUMMARY REPORT BY PRODUCT TYPE
SORTED BY CURRENT MONTH SALES
February

Product Type	Current Month Sales	Prior Month Sales	% Chg.	Year to Date Sales	Last Yr. Year to Date Sales	% Chg.
----	----	----	----	----	----	----
D	72	67	7%	360	333	8%
B	52	45	16%	260	234	11%
C	44	32	38%	220	154	43%
E	35	37	-5%	175	180	-3%
A	16	25	-36%	80	100	-20%

27.   COST-VOLUME-PROFIT ANALYSIS

FILE IDENTIFICATION AREA:

Name:
Date Created:
Filename: E27.xls

INPUT AREA:

Sales Price Per Item	=	$12.00
Variable Cost Per Item	=	8.00
Total Fixed Cost	=	$24,000

OUTPUT AREA:

Sales Price	$12.00
Variable Cost	8.00

Contribution Margin	$4.00
Fixed Cost	$24,000
Breakeven Point in Units	6,000
Breakeven Point in Dollars	$72,000

29.   COST-VOLUME-PROFIT ANALYSIS: GRAPH

FILE IDENTIFICATION AREA:

Name:
Date Created:
Filename: E29.xls   Page 1 of 2

INPUT AREA:

Sales Price Per Item	=	$12.00
Variable Cost Per Item	=	8.00
Total Fixed Cost	=	$10,000

OUTPUT AREA:

Sales Price	$12.00
Variable Cost	8.00

Contribution Margin	$4.00
Fixed Cost	$10,000
Breakeven Point in Units	2,500
Breakeven Point in Dollars	$30,000

----

29. continued

E29.xls   Page 2 of 2

DATA TO BE GRAPHED:

Units	TVC	Fixed Cost	Total Cost	Sales Rev.	Profit
0	0	10,000	10,000	0	(10,000)
1,000	8,000	10,000	18,000	12,000	(6,000)
2,000	16,000	10,000	26,000	24,000	(2,000)
3,000	24,000	10,000	34,000	36,000	2,000
4,000	32,000	10,000	42,000	48,000	6,000
5,000	40,000	10,000	50,000	60,000	10,000
6,000	48,000	10,000	58,000	72,000	14,000
7,000	56,000	10,000	66,000	84,000	18,000
8,000	64,000	10,000	74,000	96,000	22,000

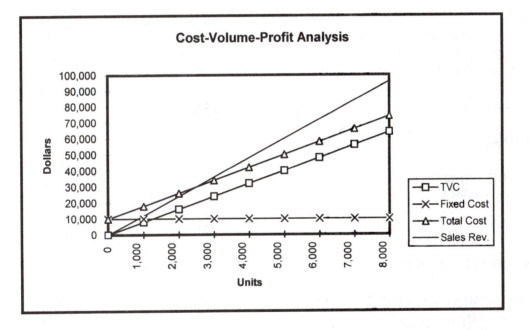

31.   FINANCIAL RATIOS

FILE IDENTIFICATION AREA:

Name:
Date Created:
Filename: E31.xls   P. 1 of 3

INPUT AREA:

	JUNIOR'S COMPUTER STORE COMPARATIVE BALANCE SHEETS 12/31/x4 and 12/31/x3	
ASSETS:	12/31/x4	12/31/x3
Cash	$1,200,000	$1,100,000
Accounts Receivable	1,780,000	550,000
Inventory	1,850,000	1,600,000
Fixed Assets (net)	8,200,000	7,200,000
Total Assets	$13,030,000	$10,450,000
LIABILITIES:		
Accounts Payable	$1,400,000	$900,000
Long Term Debt	1,730,000	430,000
Total Liabilities	$3,130,000	$1,330,000
STOCKHOLDERS EQUITY:		
Preferred stock, $100 par, 12% cum	$1,800,000	$1,800,000
Common stock, $100 par	7,000,000	7,000,000
Retained Earnings	1,100,000	320,000
Total	$9,900,000	$9,120,000
Total Liabilities + Stockholders Equity	$13,030,000	$10,450,000
Market Price of Common Stock	$109	$107

31. continued

E31.xls   P. 2 of 3

JUNIOR'S COMPUTER STORE
COMPARATIVE INCOME STATEMENTS
FYE 12/31/x4 and 12/31/x3

	12/31/x4	12/31/x3
Sales	$5,000,000	$3,300,000
Cost of Goods Sold	2,200,000	1,650,000
Gross Profit	$2,800,000	$1,650,000
Operating Expenses:		
Depreciation	$738,000	$576,000
Advertising	45,000	38,000
Other	120,000	140,000
Total Operating Expense	$903,000	$754,000
Operating Income	$1,897,000	$896,000
Interest on Long-Term Debt	80,000	80,000
Income Before Taxes	$1,817,000	$816,000
Taxes	726,800	326,400
Net Income	$1,090,200	$489,600
Dividends Declared on Preferred Stock	$220,000	$220,000
Dividends on Common Stock	290,200	299,600
Net Income to Retained Earnings	$580,000	($30,000)

NOTE: All sales are credit sales; the tax rate is 40%.

31. continued

E31.xls   P. 3 of 3

OUTPUT AREA:

------------------   19x4 Ratios:

Liquidity Ratios:
1. Current Ratio =	3.45
2. Acid-Test Ratio =	2.13

Activity Ratios:
3. Receivables Turnover =	4.29
4. Inventory Turnover =	1.28
5. Asset Turnover =	0.43

Profitability Ratios:
6. Earnings Per Share =	$12.43
7. Price to Earnings =	8.77
8. Dividend Payout =	33.35%
9. Sales Profit Margin =	21.80%
10. Return on Assets =	9.70%
11. Return on Common Stockholders Equity =	11.29%

Financial Stability Ratios:
12. Total Debt to Total Assets =	24.02%
13. Times Interest Earned =	23.71
14. Book Value Per Share =	$116
15. Cash Flow Per Share =	$26.12

FORMULAS FOR RATIOS:

Liquidity Ratios:
1. Current Ratio =	(Cur. Assets)/(Cur. Liab.)
2. Acid-Test Ratio =	(Cur. Assets - Inven. - Prep. Exp.)/(Cur. Liabilities)

Activity Ratios:
3. Receivables Turnover =	(Net Credit Sales)/(Avg. A/R)
4. Inventory Turnover =	(Cost of Gds Sold)/(Avg. Inv.)
5. Asset Turnover =	(Net Sales)/(Avg. Assets)

Profitability Ratios:
6. Earnings Per Share =	(N.I. - Pref. Div.)/(Com.Shares Out.)
7. Price to Earnings =	(Market Price per Com. Share)/(EPS)
8. Dividend Payout =	(Div. per Com. Share)/(EPS)
9. Sales Profit Margin =	(Net Income)/(Net Sales)
10. Return on Assets =	(N.I. + Int. Exp. - Tax Savings from Int.Exp.)/(Avg. Assets)
11. Return on Common Stock Equity =	(N.I. - Pref. Div.)/(Avg. Common Stock Equity)

Financial Stability Ratios:
12. Total Debt to Total Assets =	(Total Liabilities)/(Total Assets)
13. Times Interest Earned =	(Earnings before Int. and Taxes)/ (Interest Charges)
14. Book Value Per Share =	(Com. Stk Equity)/(Com. Shares O/S)
15. Cash Flow Per Share =	(N.I. + Noncash Charges)/(Com. Shares Outstanding

33.   COMMON SIZE BALANCE SHEETS

FILE IDENTIFICATION AREA:

Name:
Date Created:
Filename: E33.xls   P. 1 OF 2

INPUT AREA:

	JUNIOR'S COMPUTER STORE COMPARATIVE BALANCE SHEETS 12/31/x4 and 12/31/x3	
ASSETS:	12/31/x4	12/31/x3
Cash	$1,200,000	$1,100,000
Accounts Receivable	1,780,000	550,000
Inventory	1,850,000	1,600,000
Fixed Assets (net)	8,200,000	7,200,000
Total Assets	$13,030,000	$10,450,000
LIABILITIES:		
Accounts Payable	$1,400,000	$900,000
Long Term Debt	1,730,000	430,000
Total Liabilities	$3,130,000	$1,330,000
STOCKHOLDERS EQUITY:		
Preferred stock, $100 par, 12% cum	$1,800,000	$1,800,000
Common stock, $100 par	7,000,000	7,000,000
Retained Earnings	1,100,000	320,000
Total	$9,900,000	$9,120,000
Total Liabilities + Stockholders Equity	$13,030,000	$10,450,000

33. continued

E33.xls   **Page 2 of 2**

OUTPUT AREA:

	JUNIOR'S COMPUTER STORE COMMON SIZE BALANCE SHEETS 12/31/x4 and 12/31/x3	
ASSETS:	12/31/x4	12/31/x3
Cash	9.21%	10.53%
Accounts Receivable	13.66%	5.26%
Inventory	14.20%	15.31%
Fixed Assets (net)	62.93%	68.90%
Total Assets	100.00%	100.00%
LIABILITIES:		
Accounts Payable	10.74%	8.61%
Long Term Debt	13.28%	4.11%
Total Liabilities	24.02%	12.73%
STOCKHOLDERS EQUITY:		
Preferred stock, $100 par, 12% cum	13.81%	17.22%
Common stock, $100 par	53.72%	66.99%
Retained Earnings	8.44%	3.06%
Total	75.98%	87.27%
Total Liabilities + Stockholders Equity	100.00%	100.00%

35. FOREIGN CURRENCY TRANSLATION - CURRENT RATE METHOD

IDENTIFICATION AREA:
Filename: E35.xls   Page 1 of 2
Designer: K. Smith
Date: Aug. 18, 2001

INPUT AREA:

Adjusted Trial Balance
In Dutch Guilders (DG)
December 31, Year 4

	Debit	Credit
Cash	20,000	
Accounts Receivable	35,000	
Inventory	105,000	
Equipment	60,000	
Accum. Dep.		20,000
Accounts Payable		35,000
Bonds Payable		50,000
Revenues		120,000
General Expenses	108,000	
Depreciation Expense	8,000	
Dividends	4,000	
Common Stock		62,000
Paid-in Capital in Excess of Par		44,000
Retained Earnings		9,000
Total	340,000	340,000

Exchange Rates:

	1 DG = $___
Current Exchange Rate	1.200
Average Exchange Rate	1.250
At July 31, Year 4	1.300
At June 30, Year 1	1.000

Other: All common stock was issued on June 30, Year 1 (i.e., 6/30/Y1).
Dividends were declared and paid on July 31, Year 4.
Translated Retained Earnings at 12/31/Y3 was: $5,500

35. continued

E35.xls   Page 2 of 2

OUTPUT AREA: **SOLUTION TO E35**

Translation from Dutch Guilders to Dollars
Current Rate Method

Debits:	Dutch Guilders	Exchange Rates	U.S. Dollars
Cash	20,000	1.200	24,000
A/R	35,000	1.200	42,000
Inventory	105,000	1.200	126,000
Fixed Assets	60,000	1.200	72,000
General Expenses	108,000	1.250	135,000
Depreciation Exp.	8,000	1.250	10,000
Dividends (7/31/Y4)	4,000	1.300	5,200
Total	340,000		414,200

Credits:	Dutch Guilders	Exchange Rates	U.S. Dollars
Accum. Depreciation	20,000	1.200	24,000
A/P	35,000	1.200	42,000
Bonds Payable	50,000	1.200	60,000
Revenues	120,000	1.250	150,000
Common Stock (6/30/Y1)	62,000	1.000	62,000
Paid-in Cap. (6/30/Y1)	44,000	1.000	44,000
Retained Earnings	9,000	n.a.	5,500
Cum. Transl. Adjustment			26,700
Total	340,000		414,200

37.   FOREIGN CURRENCY TRANSLATION - CURRENT RATE METHOD

IDENTIFICATION AREA:
Filename: E37.xls   Page 1 of 2
Designer: K. Smith
Date: Aug. 18, 2001

INPUT AREA:

	Adjusted Trial Balance In British Pounds December 31, Year 8	
	Debit	Credit
Cash	72,000	
Accounts Receivable	60,000	
Inventory	136,000	
Fixed Assets	130,000	
Accum. Dep.		76,000
Accounts Payable		50,000
Bonds Payable		90,000
Revenues		172,000
General Expenses	158,000	
Depreciation Expense	10,000	
Dividends	4,000	
Common Stock		58,000
Paid-in Capital in Excess of Par		98,000
Retained Earnings		26,000
Total	570,000	570,000

Exchange Rates:

	1 BP = $___
Current Exchange Rate	3.100
Average Exchange Rate	2.900
At July 31, Year 8	2.950
At June 30, Year 1	4.000

Other:
All common stock was issued on June 30, Year 1 (i.e., 6/30/Y1).
Dividends were declared and paid on July 31, Year 8.
Translated Retained Earnings at 12/31/Y7 was: $22,600

37. continued

E37.xls   **Page 2 of 2**

OUTPUT AREA:

Translation from British Pounds to Dollars
Current Rate Method

Debits:		British Pounds	Exchange Rates	U.S. Dollars
	Cash	72,000	3.100	223,200
	A/R	60,000	3.100	186,000
	Inventory	136,000	3.100	421,600
	Fixed Assets	130,000	3.100	403,000
	General Expenses	158,000	2.900	458,200
	Depreciation Exp.	10,000	2.900	29,000
	Dividends (7/31/Y4)	4,000	2.950	11,800
Total		570,000		1,732,800

Credits:				
	Accum. Depreciation	76,000	3.100	235,600
	A/P	50,000	3.100	155,000
	Bonds Payable	90,000	3.100	279,000
	Revenues	172,000	2.900	498,800
	Common Stock (6/30/Y1)	58,000	4.000	232,000
	Paid-in Cap. (6/30/Y1)	98,000	4.000	392,000
	Retained Earnings	26,000	n.a.	22,600
	Cum. Transl. Adjustment			(82,200)
Total		570,000		1,732,800

39. FOREIGN CURRENCY TRANSLATION - TEMPORAL RATE METHOD

IDENTIFICATION AREA:
Filename: E39.xls   P. 1 of 2
Designer: K. Smith
Date: Aug. 18, 2001

Use the temporal rate method to remeasure from the currency of books and records
(i.e., British pounds) to the functional currency (i.e., U.S. dollars).

INPUT AREA:

Adjusted Trial Balance
In British Pounds
December 31, Year 4

	Debit	Credit
Cash	52,000	
Accounts Receivable	60,000	
Inventory		
(10-31-Y3)	40,000	
(7-31-Y4)	160,000	
Fixed Assets		
(6-30-Y1)	13,000	
(12-31-Y1)	65,000	
(7-31-Y2)	52,000	
Accum. Dep.		
(6-30-Y1)		8,000
(12-31-Y1)		40,000
(7-31-Y2)		32,000
Accounts Payable		43,000
Bonds Payable		160,000
Revenues		214,000
General Expenses	189,000	
Depreciation Expense		
(6-30-Y1)	1,500	
(12-31-Y1)	7,500	
(7-31-Y2)	6,000	
Dividends (7-31-Y4)	10,000	
Common Stock		
(6-30-Y1)		48,000
(1-31-Y2)		32,000
Paid-in Capital in Excess of Par		
(6-30-Y1)		30,000
(1-31-Y2)		20,000
Retained Earnings		29,000
Total	656,000	656,000

Exchange Rates:

	1 BP = $___
Current Exchange Rate	2.000
Average Exchange Rate	2.400
At July 31, Year 4	2.300
At October 31, Year 3	2.150
At July 31, Year 2	2.200
At January 31, Year 2	2.180
At December 31, Year 1	2.250
At June 30, Year 1	2.100

39. continued

E39.xls   **P. 2 of 2**

Other:

Regarding common stock, 60% was issued 6/30/Y1; 40% on 1/31/Y2.
Regarding inventory, 20% was acquired 10/31/Y3; 80% on 7/31/Y4.
Dividends were declared and paid on 7/31/Y4.
Regarding fixed assets, 10% were acquired 6/30/Y1; 50% on 12/31/Y1; and
     40% on 7/31/Y2.
Revenues and expenses were accrued evenly throughout the year.
Translated retained earnings at 12/31/Y3 was : $16,400

OUTPUT AREA: **SOLUTION TO EXERCISE 39**

Translation from British Pounds to Dollars
Current Rate Method

Debits:	British Pounds	Exchange Rates	U.S. Dollars
Cash	52,000	2.000	104,000
A/R	60,000	2.000	120,000
Inventory (10/31/Y3)	40,000	2.150	86,000
(7/31/Y4)	160,000	2.300	368,000
Fixed Assets (6/30/Y1)	13,000	2.100	27,300
(12/31/Y1)	65,000	2.250	146,250
(7/31/Y2)	52,000	2.200	114,400
General Expenses	189,000	2.400	453,600
Depreciation Exp. (6/30/Y1)	1,500	2.100	3,150
(12/31/Y1)	7,500	2.250	16,875
(7/31/Y2)	6,000	2.200	13,200
Dividends (7/31/Y4)	10,000	2.300	23,000
Total	656,000		1,475,775

Credits:	British Pounds	Exchange Rates	U.S. Dollars
Accum. Depreciation (6/30/Y1)	8,000	2.100	16,800
(12/31/Y1)	40,000	2.250	90,000
(7/31/Y2)	32,000	2.200	70,400
A/P	43,000	2.000	86,000
Bonds Payable	160,000	2.000	320,000
Revenues	214,000	2.400	513,600
Common Stock (6/30/Y1)	48,000	2.100	100,800
(1/31/Y2)	32,000	2.180	69,760
Paid-in Cap. (6/30/Y1)	30,000	2.100	63,000
(1/31/Y2)	20,000	2.180	43,600
Retained Earnings	29,000	n.a.	16,400
Cum. Transl. Adjustment			85,415
Total	656,000		1,475,775

41.   ECONOMIC IMPACT OF IMPORT QUOTA

IDENTIFICATION AREA:

Filename: E41.xls   P. 1 of 2
Designer: K. Smith
Date: Aug. 18, 1999

INPUT/OUTPUT AREA:

Use the following equation to preparing a domestic demand curve:

$$P(QD) = 120 - 10*Q$$

Use the following equations to preparing a domestic supply and a world supply curve:

$$P(QS\text{-}d) = 20 + 10*Q$$
$$P(QS\text{-}w) = 30 + 0*Q$$

Part (a): Table of Q, P(QD), P(QS-d), and P(QS-w).

Q	P(QD)	P(QS-d)	P(QS-w)
0	120	20	30
1	110	30	30
2	100	40	30
3	90	50	30
4	80	60	30
5	70	70	30
6	60	80	30
7	50	90	30
8	40	100	30
9	30	110	30
10	20	120	30

41. continued

E41.XLS   Page 2 of 2

Part (b): Graph of the domestic demand curve, domestic supply curve, world
           supply curve, and a vertical line at a quantity of 3 (quota = 3). This
           illustrates the effects of a quota.

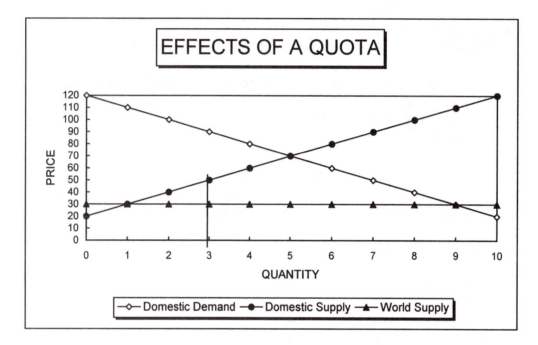

Part (c), Equilibrium:
The world market price is $30 at any quantity demanded; in other words, the
world supply curve is perfectly elastic at a price of $30. Prior to the quota,
domestic consumers could import any quantity at a price of $30. Prior to the
quota, equilibrium price was $30 and equilibrium quanitity (QD=QS) was
9 units. As a result of the quota of 3 units, equilibrium price becomes $70
and equilibrium quantity (QD=QS) becomes 5 units.

Part (d), Winners and Losers:
A domestic monopolist who can persuade the government to restrict foreign
competition will benefit. The big winners in this situation are the importers
who make huge profits at $70, instead of the world market price of $30.
Domestic producers are also able to charge $70 for their output. The
losers are the domestic consumers who must pay a price of $70 rather than
the world market price of $30. If the government auctions off the right to
import the good, then the profit would go the the federal Treasury rather than
the importer.

43.   ECONOMIC IMPACT OF A TARIFF

IDENTIFICATION AREA:

Filename: E43.xls   P. 1 of 2
Designer: K. Smith
Date: March 26, 1999

DIRECTIONS:
Use the following information and analyze the impact of a tariff.

Use the following equation to prepare a domestic demand curve:
$$P(QD) = 120 - 1*Q$$
Use the following equations to prepare a supply curve before and after the tariff is implemented. The tariff is set at $40.
$$P(QS) = 20 + 1*Q$$
$$PQS)+T = (20 + 1*Q) + T$$

Prepare the following:
  a. Table of Q (from 0 to 100, in increments of 10), P(QD), P(QS), and P(QS)+T.
  b. Graph of the demand curve (P(QD), supply curve before tariff (P(QS),
     supply curve after tariff (P(QS)+T).
  c. What is equilibrium price and quantity before and after the tariff?
  d. What is the protective effect and revenue effect of the tariff?

INPUT/OUTPUT AREA: **Solution to Exercise 43**

Part (a): Table of Q, P(QD), P(QS-d), and P(QS-w).

Q	P(QD)	P(QS)	P(QS)+T
0	120	20	60
10	110	30	70
20	100	40	80
30	90	50	90
40	80	60	100
50	70	70	110
60	60	80	120
70	50	90	130
80	40	100	140
90	30	110	150
100	20	120	160

43. continued

E43.xls   P. 2 of 2

Part (b): Graph of the demand curve, supply curve prior to the tariff, and the
          supply curve after the tariff.

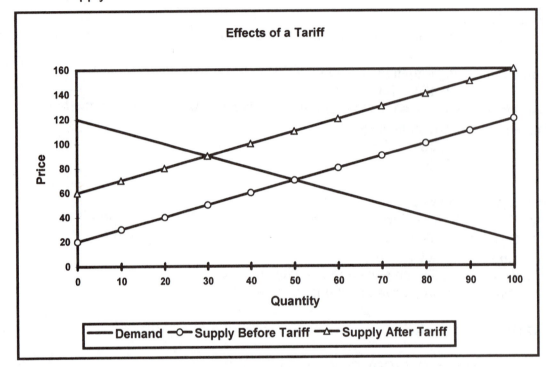

Part (c), Equilibrium:
Prior to the tariff, the equilibrium price was $70 and equilibrium quantity was 50.
After the tariff was implemented, equilibrium price is $90 and equilibrium
quantity is 30. The supply curve has shifted back to the left in the same way
that it does when a tax is imposed.

Part (d), Protective Effect and Revenue Effect:
The protective effect of a tariff is the extent to which imports are limited by its
implementation. In this way, a tariff protects domestic industry from foreign
competition. In this case, 20 units have been kept out of the market.
The revenue effect of a tariff is the amount of tax revenue it generates for
the government. In this case, the revenue effect is $1,200 ($40 * 30 units).

45.   LEASE PAYMENT

FILE IDENTIFICATION AREA:

Name:
Date Created:
Filename: E45.xls

INPUT AREA:

Initial Carrying Value (1/1/Y1): $20,000
Beginning of Term: Jan. 1, Y1
Interest Rate: 12%
Payment (Beg. 12/31/Y1): $5,548

OUTPUT AREA:

DATE	PAYMENT	INTEREST EXPENSE	AMORTIZATION	CARRYING VALUE
Jan. 1, Y1				$20,000
Dec. 31, Y1	$5,548	$2,400	$3,148	$16,852
Dec. 31, Y2	$5,548	$2,022	$3,526	$13,326
Dec. 31, Y3	$5,548	$1,599	$3,949	$9,377
Dec. 31, Y4	$5,548	$1,125	$4,423	$4,954
Dec. 31, Y5	$5,548	$594	$4,954	$0

Index

Topic	**Page No.**

Topic	**Page No.**
toolbar	6
toolbar buttons	20
Windows	3
Windows 95	3
Windows File Manager	4
Windows Program Manager	3
worksheet requirements	48